SCHOLARSHIP RECONSIDERED

SCHOLARSHIP RECONSIDERED

Priorities of the Professoriate

EXPANDED EDITION

Updated and Expanded by
Drew Moser, Todd C. Ream,
John M. Braxton, and Associates

JB JOSSEY-BASS™
A Wiley Brand

Published by Jossey-Bass
A Wiley Brand
One Montgomery Street, Suite 1000, San Francisco, CA 94104-4594—www.josseybass.com

Library of Congress Cataloging-in-Publication Data
Boyer, Ernest L., author.
Scholarship reconsidered : priorities of the professoriate / Ernest L. Boyer ; updated and expanded by Drew Moser, Todd C. Ream, John M. Braxton, and associates. – Expanded edition.
pages cm
Includes bibliographical references and index.
ISBN 978-1-118-98830-5 (pbk.), ISBN 978-1-119-00575-9 (ePDF),
ISBN 978-1-119-00586-5 (epub)
1. Education, Higher–United States. 2. College teachers–United States. 3. Learning and scholarship–United States. 4. Research–United States. I. Moser, Drew, editor. II. Ream, Todd C., editor. III. Braxton, John M., editor. IV. Title.
LA227.4.B69 2015
378.73–dc23
2015029127

Cover design by Wiley

Cover image: Abstract Background © iStock.com/Gile68, Texture Paper © iStock.com/Malsveta

Printed in the United States of America

EXPANDED EDITION
PB Printing 10 9 8 7 6 5

CONTENTS

ABOUT ERNEST L. BOYER

Ernest L. Boyer (1928–1995) served as the president of the Carnegie Foundation for the Advancement of Teaching, the United States Commissioner of Education, the chancellor of the State University of New York, and held a wide variety of other faculty and administrative roles at colleges and universities such as the University of California, Santa Barbara, and Upland College. During his time as president of the Carnegie Foundation, Boyer and his colleagues produced a wide array of influential reports on topics ranging from early childhood education to an international study of the professoriate. The original edition of *Scholarship Reconsidered* was produced during that time.

Boyer was raised in Dayton, Ohio, and earned his undergraduate degree at Greenville College in Greenville, Illinois. Following graduation, he and his wife, Katherine Boyer, moved to Orlando, Florida, where Boyer served as pastor of a Brethren in Christ church. The Boyers then moved to Southern California, where Boyer began his career in education as an administrator at Upland College. After earning his PhD at the University of Southern California, Boyer conducted postdoctoral work at the University of Iowa.

After Boyer lost a three-year battle with lymphoma in 1995, William H. Honan wrote in the *New York Times* that Boyer had "never tired of his role as an evangelist of education." Through his later years he remained a sought-after speaker on higher and adult education and the importance of civics education. Boyer also held some 140 honorary degrees and numerous awards, including the Charles Frankel Prize in the Humanities, the Horatio Alger Award, and the Britannica Achievement in Life Award.

ABOUT THE EDITORS

Drew Moser (PhD, Indiana State University) is dean of experiential learning and associate professor of higher education at Taylor University. Drew has written extensively on the life and legacy of Ernest Boyer and is coauthoring (with Todd C. Ream) *Ernest L. Boyer: A Cultural Biography* for SUNY Press. He is also co-director of *The Vocation in College Project*, a multiphased research project examining vocation formation in the college student experience. Drew writes frequently on his website, HigherEdReconsidered.com, and can be reached via his Twitter account, @drewmoser.

Todd C. Ream (PhD, Pennsylvania State University) is professor of higher education at Taylor University and a research fellow with the Institute for Studies of Religion at Baylor University. Todd has contributed articles, editorials, interviews, and reviews to a wide range of journals, magazines, and newspapers. His books include *Christian Faith and Scholarship: An Exploration of Contemporary Developments* (with Perry L. Glanzer, Jossey-Bass); *Christianity and Moral Identity in Higher Education* (with Perry L. Glanzer, Palgrave Macmillan); *A Parent's Guide to the Christian College: Supporting Your Child's Mind and Spirit during the College Years* (with Timothy W. Herrmann and C. Skip Trudeau, Abilene Christian University Press); and *The Idea of a Christian College: A Reexamination for Today's University* (with Perry L. Glanzer, Cascade Books). Todd also serves as the book review editor (with Perry L. Glanzer) for *Christian Scholar's Review.*

John M. Braxton (EdD, Pennsylvania State University) is professor of education in the Higher Education Leadership and Policy Program at Vanderbilt University. His research interests center on the study of college and university faculty members and on the college student experience. He has contributed publications in the form of refereed journals, book chapters, edited books, and books. His books include *Professors Behaving Badly: Faculty Misconduct in Graduate Education* (Johns Hopkins University Press); *Faculty Misconduct in Collegiate Teaching* (with Alan E. Bayer, Johns Hopkins University Press); *Rethinking College Student Retention* (with William R. Doyle and associates, Jossey-Bass); *Understanding and Reducing College Student Departure* (with Amy S. Hirschy and Shederick A. McClendon, Jossey-Bass); and *Institutionalizing a Broader View of Scholarship through Boyer's Four Domains* (with William Luckey and Patricia Helland, Jossey-Bass). John currently serves as editor of the *Journal of College Student Development* and as associate editor (faculty issues) for *Higher Education: A Handbook of Theory and Research* (Springer). He is also a past president of the Association for the Study of Higher Education.

ABOUT THE CONTRIBUTORS

Ann E. Austin (PhD, University of Michigan) is professor of higher, adult, and lifelong education at Michigan State University, where she held the Mildred B. Erickson Distinguished Chair from 2005 to 2008 and again in 2014. Beginning in January 2015, she is serving as a program director in the Division of Undergraduate Education at the National Science Foundation. Her research concerns faculty careers and professional development, teaching and learning in higher education, the academic workplace, organizational change, and doctoral education. She is a fellow of the American Educational Research Association and past president of the Association for the Study of Higher Education, and a Fulbright Fellow in South Africa (1998). Ann has published extensively, including *Educating Integrated Professionals: Theory and Practice on Preparation for the Professoriate* (with Carol L. Colbeck and KerryAnn O'Meara, Jossey-Bass); *Rethinking Faculty Work: Higher Education's Strategic Imperative* (with Judith M. Gappa and Andrea G. Trice, Jossey-Bass); and *Paths to the Professoriate: Strategies for Enriching the Preparation of Future Faculty* (with Donald H. Wulff, Jossey-Bass).

Andrea L. Beach (PhD, Michigan State University) is associate professor of educational leadership, research, and technology and director of faculty development at Western Michigan University. Her research centers on organizational change in higher education, support of innovation in teaching and learning, faculty learning communities, and faculty development as a change lever. She has been primary investigator and co-primary investigator on NSF-funded grants that have produced several articles on instructional change strategies. She is a coauthor of *Creating the Future of Faculty Development: Learning from the Past, Understanding the Present* (Jossey-Bass) and is currently lead author on a ten-year follow-up to that work, *Faculty Development in the Age of Evidence.* She is most recently director of a $3.2 million project funded by the US Department of Education's First in the World program to undertake, document, and measure outcomes of institutional transformation aimed at improving the persistence and academic success of students from low-income families and disadvantaged backgrounds.

Mary Taylor Huber (PhD, University of Pittsburgh) is senior scholar emerita at the Carnegie Foundation for the Advancement of Teaching. Since joining the foundation in 1985, she has written widely on cultures of teaching in higher education, integrative learning, and faculty member rewards and roles. Author of the influential Carnegie Foundation report, *Scholarship Assessed: Evaluation of the Professoriate* (with Charles E. Glassick and Gene I. Maeroff, Jossey-Bass), her recent books include *Disciplinary Styles in the Scholarship of Teaching and Learning* (with Sherwyn P. Morreale, Stylus Publishing); *Balancing Acts: The Scholarship of Teaching and Learning in Academic Careers* (Stylus Publishing); *The Advancement of Learning: Building the Teaching Commons* (with Pat Hutchings, Jossey-Bass); and *The Scholarship of Teaching and Learning Reconsidered: Institutional Integration and Impact* (with Pat Hutchings and Anthony Ciccone, Jossey-Bass).

Melissa McDaniels (PhD, Michigan State University) is assistant dean of the graduate school and director of the Teaching Assistant Program at Michigan State University. McDaniels has more than twenty years of experience in graduate student and faculty development, undergraduate and graduate teaching, and learning and organizational change. From 2008 to 2012, McDaniels served as director of Michigan State University's NSF ADVANCE Grant (in the Office of the Provost), where she spearheaded the institution's efforts to diversify the faculty in science, technology, engineering, and mathematics (STEM) fields. Prior to 2008, she held full-time positions at Northeastern University, Boston College, and the National Geographic Society. She has consulted domestically and internationally on topics related to programmatic and learning assessment in higher education, graduate student research capacity development, and graduate student teaching development. The primary focus of McDaniels's research is graduate student, postdoctoral, and faculty professional development.

KerryAnn O'Meara (PhD, University of Maryland) is professor of higher education, co-principal investigator, and co-director of the Advance Program, and an affiliate faculty member in women's studies at the University of Maryland. KerryAnn spent two years working as a research associate at Harvard University's Project on Faculty Appointments and six years on the faculty at the University of Massachusetts Amherst before joining the faculty at the University of Maryland College Park in fall 2007. KerryAnn's scholarship explores organizing practices that support diverse faculty members and diverse forms of scholarship, especially within academic reward systems, faculty development, and in the careers of women and engaged scholars. She has consulted with individual campuses and nationally since 2000 on ways to reform promotion and tenure policies to acknowledge broader definitions of scholarship, including engaged scholarship.

Cynthia A. Wells (PhD, Ohio State University) is assistant professor of higher education, director of the Ernest L. Boyer Center, and program director for the master of arts in higher education program at Messiah College. Cynthia served for several years as a fellow in the Boyer Center and in that capacity provided leadership for the Boyer Partnership Assessment Project—a Fund for the Improvement of Post-secondary Education (FIPSE) funded research project that examined student affairs and academic affairs partnership programs. Her current scholarship focuses on general education and common learning, vocational formation in higher education, and personal narrative pedagogy. Cynthia recently served as a NetVUE Scholar through the Council of Independent College's Network for Vocation in Undergraduate Education (NetVUE).

EDITORS' ACKNOWLEDGMENTS

Any record of the debts we owe must first and foremost begin with Ernest L. Boyer and his family, in particular his wife, Kay, and their four children—Ernie Jr., Beverly, Craig, and Paul. Ernest Boyer's leadership in education contributed mightily to the vision, completion, and eventual success of *Scholarship Reconsidered.* Those ideas, combined with his charisma and relentless work ethic, resulted in seismic changes in academe. This work does, and always will, belong to him and the colleagues who assisted him with it. Through many subsequent efforts Kay and the Boyer children have sought to honor their husband and father through their own efforts to serve the needs of a wide variety of people in places as different as New Hampshire, California, and Belize.

This edition of Boyer's work would have proved impossible without the wisdom offered by its contributors—Ann Austin, Andrea Beach, Mary Taylor Huber, Melissa McDaniels, KerryAnn O'Meara, and Cynthia Wells. Thank you for your efforts and for your willingness to share your wisdom with a new generation of audience members for *Scholarship Reconsidered.* In the face of so many declension narratives attacking higher education, we find hope that the academy is led by such bright, committed scholars.

Our colleagues on our own respective campuses continue to also serve as a means of hope. Drew and Todd specifically want to thank colleagues at Taylor University: Skip Trudeau, Tim Herrmann, Scott Gaier,

Steve Bedi, Dan Bowell, Bill Ringenberg, Tom Jones, Felicia Case, Steve Morley, Kevin Diller, Jess Fankhauser, Jeff Aupperle, Kelly Yordy, Heather Sandlin, and Emily Bryan. We thank our Taylor colleagues for embodying the best of what Boyer envisioned for academic community. John offers heartfelt thanks to his colleagues in the Association for the Study of Higher Education community along with his colleagues in the Peabody School of Education at Vanderbilt University.

Our families are the ones to whom we likely owe the greatest debt. Scholarship is a consuming endeavor with ill-defined boundaries and, at times, uncertain rewards. Through it all, our families have been unwavering in their support and encouragement.

From Drew: Thanks to my wife, Rebekah, for her love and care throughout this process. To echo Ernest Boyer's words to his spouse, Kay, in *High School*, "Words fail." Thanks to my children, Benjamin, Eloisa, Samuel, Stella, and William. As the beginning of your own higher education journeys draws near, with apparent acceleration, I am increasingly aware of the very personal nature of my work. That work in higher education, symbolized in part by this book, is for you and your future. Thank you for your inspiration, your imagination, and your unconditional love for your father.

From Todd: My thanks to my wife, Sara, for the gracious ways she keeps me focused on what is truly important. To our children, Addison and Ashley, who draw closer every day to being the direct recipients of what Boyer envisioned for higher education–when you arrive, I will be filled with the mixed feelings of pride over your accomplishments and sorrow over knowing experiences such as our Saturday conversations over breakfast (for Addison) and sushi (for Ashley) will be reserved for your precious trips home. In between those trips, I hope the best of Boyer's words find their way to educators striving to cultivate your created potential.

From John: Thanks to my wife, Dr. Ellen M. Brier.

We now entrust Boyer's words into your hands—a new generation of readers. We hope that anything we and our fellow contributors offer here only enhances your appreciation of Boyer's ideas. In order to appreciate those ideas, please remember Boyer did not intend for them to be passively accepted but to become part of a lively dialogue that draws together colleagues who are willing to disagree without succumbing to being disagreeable. Please take, hold, read, discuss, and, if needed, discuss again.

Drew Moser
Todd C. Ream
John M. Braxton

A NOTE TO THE READER

In today's seemingly frenetic publishing world, it is rare to find a work that persists beyond its first printing. The year 2015 marks the twenty-fifth anniversary of *Scholarship Reconsidered: Priorities of the Professoriate* by Ernest L. Boyer (1928–1995). Boyer, an internationally known educational leader, was best known for his leadership as chancellor of the SUNY system (1971–1977), United States Commissioner of Education (1977–1979), and president of the Carnegie Foundation for the Advancement of Teaching (1979–1995). As his stature as an educational leader became more pronounced, so did his inclination and ability to draw scholars together. This is arguably best evidenced in *Scholarship Reconsidered.*

Written by Boyer and his Carnegie Foundation colleagues (most notably Eugene Rice), *Scholarship Reconsidered* has sold more than thirty-five thousand copies since Jossey-Bass took over its publication in 1997. It has also been cited over 6,675 times, according to Google Scholar. Sales and citations aside, it remains a text germane to the conversation about scholarship in the academy. When *Scholarship Reconsidered* was released in 1990, it sparked conversations that have only grown in strength and complexity to this day. These conversations expanded beyond the traditional research agenda to include four domains: application, discovery, integration, and teaching. In honor of this work's twenty-fifth anniversary, what you hold in your hands is an edition that not only critically engages that legacy but also offers space for speculation about its future. Given the challenges and opportunities facing higher education today, we believe Boyer's work will prove to be even more relevant over the course of the next quarter century.

Determining the veracity of this claim of Boyer's continued relevance is, in many ways, up to you, your colleagues, and the communities you serve. The essays provided offer you a host of ways to think through the legacy of *Scholarship Reconsidered* and its relevance to your work as higher education scholars, administrators, and policy makers.

The text begins, appropriately, with a foreword from Mary Taylor Huber, entitled "*Scholarship Reconsidered*'s Influence in Later Carnegie Foundation Work." Huber was with the Carnegie Foundation as a senior scholar for the duration of Boyer's tenure as president. She was a pivotal voice in Carnegie Foundation work and continued the conversation *Scholarship Reconsidered* launched after Boyer's untimely death in 1995. She is perhaps best positioned to write on the impact of *Scholarship Reconsidered* on the Carnegie Foundation's later work. Think of Huber's contribution as primary source account of *Scholarship Reconsidered*'s development and impact, providing a Carnegie Foundation perspective to serve as a contextual backdrop for assessing the report's influence over the past twenty-five years. This foreword is followed by five chapters from Boyer scholars that focus this exploration through five important lenses: history, faculty development, institutional type and academic discipline, doctoral and professional education, and promotion and tenure.

The first chapter, "The Origins of *Scholarship Reconsidered*," is authored by two of us (Drew Moser and Todd C. Ream). It examines the lesser known influences and experiences that shaped Ernest Boyer's development of *Scholarship Reconsidered*. It chronicles his early life and career and the context, events, and key individuals that shaped this new domain of scholarship.

The second chapter, authored by Andrea L. Beach, is titled "Boyer's Impact on Faculty Development." It provides a helpful perspective into the role *Scholarship Reconsidered* played in the emergence of the scholarship of teaching and learning (SoTL) and faculty development. It also highlights potential trajectories for these movements into the future.

Third, John M. Braxton contributes "The Influence of *Scholarship Reconsidered* on Institutional Types and Academic Disciplines." It is a technical examination of how institutions and disciplines have responded to the expansive view of scholarship provided in *Scholarship Reconsidered*.

By analyzing scholarly activity through the delineation of *Scholarship Reconsidered*'s four domains, you can read the extent to which certain types of institutions and certain academic disciplines have embraced this framework.

Ann E. Austin and Melissa McDaniels collaborated on this book's fourth chapter, "*Scholarship Reconsidered*'s Impact on Doctoral and Professional Education." Austin and McDaniels explore the influence of *Scholarship Reconsidered* on doctoral education, with specific attention to hallmark professional programs such as law and medicine. They provide important insight into *Scholarship Reconsidered*'s relevance for these modes of learning.

The fifth chapter, written by KerryAnn O'Meara, examines what is often the most contentious conversation surrounding *Scholarship Reconsidered*: promotion and tenure. "How *Scholarship Reconsidered* Disrupted the Promotion and Tenure System" argues for the prominent place this work holds in the revision of promotion and tenure guidelines over the past twenty-five years. O'Meara explores how Boyer provided a new language for a new approach to promotion and tenure.

Last, Cynthia A. Wells, director of the Ernest L. Boyer Center at Messiah College, provides an afterword at the end of expanded edition. Appropriately titled "Advancing the Conversation around *Scholarship Reconsidered*," Wells conducts the many voices of this edition into a chorus that collectively assesses the relevance of Ernest L. Boyer's views to the present and future of higher education. She also provides an understanding of how the Ernest L. Boyer Center seeks to continue the dialogue *Scholarship Reconsidered* began in 1990.

Twenty-five years provides many avenues for exploration, too many to consider in one book. Collectively, these seven contributions attempt to examine twenty-five years of influence, and in so doing, refocus our view of *Scholarship Reconsidered* for many years to come. The text of *Scholarship Reconsidered*, of course, is included in this book and remains unchanged. However, as with the first twenty-five years, Boyer's work is at its best when it is read and debated by communities of scholars. To support such efforts, we also provided a discussion guide. In the end, however, we leave it up to you to decide how to use this book. Some may read it from cover to cover and then add their own questions to the discussion guide. Some may read only the essays and selections from the text that prove to be most relevant to them at a particular point in time. Others may find its use as a reference work to prove most beneficial. Regardless, we hope you find that engaging this work is of great benefit to your vocation as a scholar. Ernest L. Boyer is perhaps remembered most for being a scholar of scholars. He consistently tried to determine how to best draw scholars together into relationships that would enable them to flourish. It is our hope that this new book cultivates generative, robust conversations among scholars on the very nature of scholarship.

Drew Moser
Todd C. Ream
John M. Braxton

FOREWORD

Scholarship Reconsidered's Influence in Later Carnegie Foundation Work

Mary Taylor Huber

We believe the time has come to move beyond the tired old "teaching versus research" debate and give the familiar and honorable term "scholarship" a broader, more capacious meaning, one that brings legitimacy to the full scope of academic work.[1]

The publication of *Scholarship Reconsidered: Priorities of the Professoriate* in 1990 propelled Ernest L. Boyer, author of the report and president of the Carnegie Foundation for the Advancement of Teaching, onto another of his many ambitious speaking tours. Keynoting events on campuses and at conferences around the country, Boyer would speak engagingly and persuasively about *Scholarship Reconsidered*'s major theme. As suggested in my epigraph, Boyer believed that the term "scholarship" had come to be too narrowly interpreted in American higher education. Only by broadening its scope beyond basic research could colleges and universities fulfill their wide range of institutional commitments.

The ideas presented in *Scholarship Reconsidered* have enjoyed a long history as a potent inspiration for reform—but not entirely on their own. What force they've had has been enhanced by the work of many colleagues who have elaborated on their meaning, explored ways to institutionalize them, and provided exemplars of what it looks like to embrace a broader understanding of the scope of scholarly work. Not least among these efforts has been continuing work at the Carnegie Foundation itself—my topic in this foreword. As a member of the teams that Boyer assembled at the Carnegie Foundation to help with *Scholarship Reconsidered* and its follow-up report *Scholarship Assessed*,[2] and as one who continued at Carnegie in President Lee Shulman's Carnegie Academy for the Scholarship of Teaching and Learning,[3] I look at Carnegie's role in keeping *Scholarship Reconsidered* vital and alive.

Let's go back to the late 1980s, when formal work on *Scholarship Reconsidered* began. Higher education was at a crossroads. After years of explosive growth in the 1950s and 1960s, American colleges and universities were suffering from a decline in public confidence. With the Second World War, the Cold War, and the social programs of the Great Society receding into the past, academic scholarship no longer wore the halo of public service. Yet rewards increasingly flowed to institutions and individuals engaged in ever-more-specialized research, giving little support to developing other kinds of scholarship that would prove increasingly important in the years to come. What about the growing needs of society for expertise in clinical work and community development? What about connecting the results of ever-more-specialized research and giving academic knowledge a wider public address? What about the growing challenge of educating a more diverse set of students in an era of requiring ever-higher levels of academic preparation?

Scholarship Reconsidered argued that higher education's working definition of academic scholarship had become too narrow to effectively address these questions and proposed that the notion of scholarship be broadened to bring "legitimacy to the full scope of academic work."[4] As Boyer went on to explain:

> Surely scholarship means engaging in original research. But the work of the scholar also means stepping back from one's investigation, looking for connections, building bridges between theory and practice, and communicating one's knowledge effectively to students. Specifically, we conclude that the work of the professoriate might be thought of as having four separate, yet overlapping, functions. These are: the scholarship of discovery; the scholarship of integration; the scholarship of application; and the scholarship of teaching.[5]

Although *Scholarship Reconsidered* provided only brief sketches of these four functions, the idea of rethinking faculty member roles and rewards in terms of a "broader, more capacious" notion of "scholarship" caught the attention of reformers across higher education. The book's impact was amplified in forums provided over the next decade by the American Association for Higher Education, where leaders from campuses across the country exchanged ideas about campus policies and practices that might encourage and support the "newer" scholarships suggested in Boyer's report. *Scholarship Reconsidered* had resonance, too, at the Carnegie Foundation for the Advancement of Teaching, where later work elaborated several of Boyer's themes and took them in new directions—some falling closer and some farther from the proverbial tree.

Boyer himself was aware that there was more work to be done. Audiences at his talks on *Scholarship Reconsidered* were clearly intrigued by the general idea, but they were also puzzled by (and some were even dismissive of) the particulars. The "scholarship of discovery" posed no real problem if understood as a gloss for "original research." But what was the justification for using the term "scholarship" to refer to application (now commonly referred to as "engagement"), integration, and, especially, teaching? And if, indeed, some work in these areas could be seen as scholarly, how could its quality be evaluated?

Boyer returned from these trips inspired. And in no time at all, plans took shape for the follow-up report, *Scholarship Assessed: Evaluation of the Professoriate.* We began with a survey of provosts of four-year institutions, which established that colleges and universities were already in the midst of rethinking their systems of faculty member roles and rewards. Recognizing that revising formal guidelines can be a lengthy process, we also asked them to send us copies of reports emerging from their campus deliberations, and these too suggested that a vigorous conversation was underway and that *Scholarship Reconsidered* was playing a role in shaping that debate.

Drafting the new report began with special attention to identifying standards that could be helpful in assessing the quality of particular examples of academic work. Aided by our study of guidelines used by campuses, scholarly journals, university presses, granting agencies, and the like, we identified a set of six standards that were widely used across disciplines to evaluate basic research, applied work, interdisciplinary projects, and teaching. Together, these standards map a common arc of intellectual endeavor: clear goals, adequate preparation, appropriate methods, significant results, effective presentation, and reflective critique. With appropriate adjustments, we argued, these standards could be applied equally well to the four kinds of scholarship identified in *Scholarship Reconsidered.*

Boyer was able to present this idea in a speech at the American Association for Higher Education in early 1995 but passed away before *Scholarship Assessed* could be completed. Charles Glassick, Gene Maeroff, and I continued to work on the book, expanding its scope to address the standards' implications for documenting scholarship and establishing a trustworthy process of evaluation. Published in 1997, many readers found the standards we proposed useful in thinking through what made a piece of work scholarly. *Scholarship Assessed* added a level of specificity to the broad brushstrokes of Boyer's earlier book, contributing to the vigorous development both in theory and in practice of all the "new" scholarships in the years that followed.

Indeed, when Carnegie's new president, Lee Shulman, took office in fall 1997, one of his major lines of work was to further develop the idea of a scholarship of teaching. Through the auspices of the Cultures of Teaching program (1998–2003) and the Carnegie Academy for the Scholarship of Teaching, or CASTL (1998–2009), we explored how this work was playing out in the disciplines, in academic careers, and on campuses. CASTL, in particular, supported the development of leadership for the scholarship of teaching and learning through a national fellowship program for individual scholars, and separate programs for disciplinary associations and campuses. Carnegie was also influential in the formation of the International Society for the Scholarship of Teaching and Learning (ISSoTL), which continues as a major forum for exchange among practitioners and advocates for this work.

Throughout this period, *Scholarship Reconsidered* and *Scholarship Assessed* grounded the effort historically. These books had introduced some of the language and ideas that helped map a new path for college and university teaching. They connected that path to those being cleared by participants in the other new scholarships (integration, especially interdisciplinary work; application, now better known as the scholarship of engagement; and even the older one, the scholarship of discovery). It may not be too much to say that they also helped leaders in all these pursuits to keep an eye on the larger prize: how the priorities of the professoriate can be better aligned with the full range of missions of higher education. This was what had inspired Boyer, with the help of those of us privileged to work with him, to write *Scholarship Reconsidered* in the first place.

To be sure, times have changed. The professoriate is no longer the predominantly tenure-track career that it once was, nor is the professoriate as singlehandedly responsible for fulfilling higher education's mission as once it had been. Yet this does not mean that the capacious vision of scholarship proposed by *Scholarship Reconsidered* is less relevant. Quite the opposite. Over the last twenty-five years of effort by faculty members, students, and other academic professionals, work that is not strictly speaking (or only) the scholarship of discovery has gained understanding and respect, developed strong communities of practice, and produced extraordinary results.

The Carnegie Foundation for the Advancement of Teaching has moved on to other programs and priorities, as foundations do. But for over twenty years, the Carnegie Foundation remained active in the field, publishing reports, designing programs, developing leadership, and convening participants in the effort to broaden and deepen the range of scholarly academic work. This ensured that Ernest Boyer's, although likely the first, was not the only influential and inspiring voice to urge colleagues to think about the possibilities opened up by thinking more capaciously about scholarship.

PART ONE

THE IMPACT OF *SCHOLARSHIP RECONSIDERED* ON TODAY'S ACADEMY

THE ORIGINS OF *SCHOLARSHIP RECONSIDERED*

Drew Moser and Todd C. Ream

Ernest L. Boyer became a household name in the 1980s and 1990s as he was a go-to public intellectual on all matters of education. His rise to prominence from SUNY chancellor to US Commissioner of Education under President Carter to president of the Carnegie Foundation is well known. Likewise, his most famous published work, *Scholarship Reconsidered: Priorities of the Professoriate,*[1] persists in the academy, evidenced by citations and sales. What is lesser known is the convergence of influences and life experiences that informed *Scholarship Reconsidered.* This essay chronicles these lesser-known details, exploring elements of Boyer's early life and his leadership style that shaped one of the most popular works in higher education literature. It addresses formative family influences, humble religious and academic beginnings, and a higher education landscape hungry for new ideas on scholarship.

Scholarship Reconsidered was a timely, albeit controversial, report. Ever the educational populist, Ernest L. Boyer desired that the practice of scholarship be a focus of national discussion, reaching well beyond the ivory tower. In addition, the Carnegie Foundation's *Campus Life*[2] report revealed that the current use of time by faculty members was a significant hindrance to the type of campus community Boyer envisioned. He lamented the "publish-or-perish" reality faculty members faced and challenged the nation to reconsider the definition of scholarship.

Original research was formally introduced to American higher education in the latter half of the 1800s and quickly became the focus of the professoriate at a number of universities, often at the expense of teaching and service. Boyer pointed his audience back to scholars who predated modern universities, reminding his audience that scholarship was once measured by the ability to think, learn, and communicate. Reports such as *Campus Life* and *Scholarship Reconsidered* also revealed the dissonance between what faculty members valued and the reward structure that measured their efforts. In particular, the majority of faculty members truly desired to teach and spend time interacting with students. The dominant structure of the modern university, however, rewarded faculty members who successfully removed themselves from the classroom (often to be replaced by graduate assistants) to spend more time on research.

Boyer's previous speeches and writing on scholarship argued the university, or at least its most influential iteration, the research university, embraced a narrow view of scholarship. How can scholarship simply be evidenced by publications? By looking back into history as well as forward into the future, Boyer then proposed a broader vision where "the work of the scholar also means stepping back from one's investigation, looking for connections, building bridges between theory and practice, and communicating one's knowledge effectively to students."[3]

After experiencing grinding economic recessions during his time at SUNY and the United States Office of Education, Boyer steered the resources and expertise of the Carnegie Foundation toward addressing the public's growing demand for college faculty members to be accountable to powers other than themselves. At the same time, those same faculty members were growing more disillusioned with their own vocational culture. Laments over the demise of the academy were surfacing at that time in greater numbers and with greater force. For example, a work such as Alan Bloom's *The Closing of the American Mind*[4] was a cultural bombshell. If released now, however, Bloom's work would likely find itself competing with titles in what has become a well-established genre.

Although these details are known to the majority of higher education scholars, leaders, and policy makers, a number of other critical influences on Boyer and *Scholarship Reconsidered* deserve further exploration. Boyer's childhood and early life, which are less well known, played a vital role in shaping the type of educational leader that made Boyer so admired. For starters, he was not the traditional public intellectual. He came from humble beginnings with an educational background to match. This very background and subsequent leadership style also inspired and frustrated individuals who worked with him.

In particular, Boyer was a tireless worker and expected those around him to maintain his frenetic pace. He surrounded himself with brilliant scholars who provided the Carnegie Foundation with compelling research reports that usually carried one name as the author—Ernest L. Boyer. This constituency of one proved somewhat controversial but effective. It brought with it the full force of Boyer's dogged work ethic, charismatic persona, and brand-name recognition. Together they were the recipe for one of the best-selling works in the history of American higher education.

To understand what made *Scholarship Reconsidered* so unique, one must consider the individuals who had a pronounced influence on Ernest Boyer; the Rev. William Boyer, Ernest Boyer's paternal grandfather, was one such influence. Later in life, when Ernest was a much sought-after speaker, he would often refer to his grandfather as the most important person in his childhood. In particular, William Boyer became known for his commitment to service. A minister in Dayton, Ohio, William founded and led the Dayton Mission for thirty-three years. The residents of Dayton, who depended in many ways on the mission's charity, were "a part of Ernie's life. . . ."[5] It was at the Dayton Mission that Ernest encountered poverty and suffering. He attended services multiple times per week, worshipping with and serving people from all walks of life.

From his grandfather, Ernest Boyer also developed an appreciation for the power of words. He admired his grandfather immensely for his compassionate spirit, his way with children, and his ability to listen. In his own words, "Grandpa taught me by example lessons I could not have learned in any classroom. He taught me that God is central to all of life, and he taught me to be truly human, one must serve."[6] William Boyer's influence on his grandson was so profound that Ernest Boyer sought to integrate service into every leadership position he held.

Boyer's first academic post was at a small, now defunct, church-related, liberal arts college in Southern California then known as Upland College. Upland provided him with an income while he earned his PhD at the University of Southern California. The college was a sister school to his alma mater, Messiah College, a Brethren-in-Christ-affiliated college in Pennsylvania. At Upland, Boyer devoted himself to the tight-knit yet fledgling institution. He gradually rose through the faculty ranks, spending two years as an instructor, two as an assistant professor and department chair, and five as academic dean, leading the institution to accreditation. In particular, Upland's vibrant campus community, a campus that extended well beyond the classroom, left a profound impact on Boyer.

In particular, Boyer's experience hardened his resolve to allow such schools a seat at the table of American higher education. Eager to replicate the accreditation success, Boyer and Upland's president, John Martin, were instrumental in the founding of the Council for the Advancement of Small Colleges, a group that helped small colleges navigate through the accreditation process. They coached small college administrators and lobbied accrediting bodies to not only consider classic metrics but also to give weight to what their graduates contributed to the world.[7] As a result of the council's efforts, ninety small colleges received accreditation, including Boyer's alma mater, Messiah College.

Ironically, as Upland's fiscal strength waned, Boyer's career began to soar. After a few posts in California's public higher education system, Boyer followed his mentor, Sam Gould, to Albany, New York, and the State University of New York (SUNY). Boyer eventually became chancellor of the SUNY system at the age of forty-two and began to place his own stamp on the largest, most complex state system in the country at that time.

While in Albany, Boyer faced a set of challenges comparable to what we face today—the need to increase access and student learning with fewer and fewer resources. Part of his answer was to create structures such as Empire State College, initially a campusless institution, now multi-site and virtual, that served as an early template for adult education and degree completion. Even today, Empire State's mission is to "use innovative, alternative and flexible approaches to higher education that transform people and communities by providing rigorous programs that connect individuals' unique and diverse lives to their personal learning goals."[8] Such efforts drew heavily on the emerging realities of the college student experience and the phenomenon now referred to as adjunct professors.

When looking back at Boyer's writings from that time, a quick survey reveals a convergence of his key philosophical tenets of education: connectedness, service, language, and teaching. Boyer insisted on viewing education in an integrated, holistic manner. If these attributes are the building blocks of a quality education, they must have an impact on scholarship within college education. In essence, scholarship must have a connection to a community. Scholarship for scholarship's sake was not an option. It must serve the common good and thus must use language effectively to foster learning. Such attributes reflect the essence of Boyer's call for an education of coherence.

After ten years at the helm in the SUNY system, Boyer was appointed United States Commissioner of Education by President Jimmy Carter in 1977. After two frustrating years in Washington, Boyer accepted his dream job as president of the Carnegie Foundation for the Advancement of Teaching—a tenure that began in 1979 and would end with his untimely death in 1995. He succeeded Clark Kerr, who had hired scholars such as Art Levine. Boyer thus inherited the Carnegie Foundation's resources, library, and rising array of scholars. Boyer placed the foundation's headquarters in Princeton, New Jersey, because of its proximity to government agencies, money, and East Coast media outlets. Levine recalls, "He [Boyer] is probably the smartest person I've ever worked with in my life. Also the most difficult . . ." (personal communication, June 3, 2014).

Boyer's strategic, sharp intellect coupled with his tireless work ethic produced a decade of important reports, such as *A Quest for Common Learning* (with Art Levine, on general education); *High School: A Report on Secondary Education in America*; *College: The Undergraduate Experience in America*; and *Campus Life: In Search of Community*.[9] These reports were read and considered, but none to the level of *Scholarship Reconsidered*.

In the late 1980s, a close friend of Boyer's, Dick Martin, handed Boyer some writings by a rising education scholar by the name of Eugene Rice. Rice, then a professor of sociology and religion at the University of the Pacific, was beginning to unfold some innovative ideas about the academic profession. Boyer was so compelled that he convinced Rice to join the Carnegie Foundation as a senior fellow in 1988 (Rice, personal communication, April 15, 2014).

At the time, Rice was already years into working on a project called *The New American Scholar*. According to Rice (personal communication, April 15, 2014), Boyer invited him to finish his book at the Carnegie Foundation. Rice would then spend two years at the foundation before accepting a post at Antioch College. He left his *New American Scholar* manuscript at the foundation with the expectation that it would be published as a collaborative effort between Rice and Boyer.

At this point the origins of *Scholarship Reconsidered* provide a case study in the differences between higher education and the philanthropic world. Boyer gave the keynote address at the annual meeting of the American Association of Higher Education, an address entitled "The New American Scholar," borrowing heavily from Rice's work.[10] This would be considered inappropriate by some in academic circles. Yet it points to a more commonly held philanthropic approach: the constituency of one. Rice, a scholar by trade, likely envisioned his work for the foundation as something explicitly attributed to him. However, foundations often operate with a different understanding. In particular, Boyer believed the foundation ought to speak with one voice. To this end, Rice was sufficiently forewarned prior to joining the Carnegie Foundation of Boyer's "one voice" mentality (Rice, personal communication, April 15, 2014).

Though controversial, Boyer's approach had the intended effect and Rice's work likely had more impact because of Boyer's approach. Rice remarked, "In fact *Scholarship Reconsidered* or *The New American Scholar* had more impact because he did what he did.... But I think there is a lot to be said for Ernie's approach and the need for one voice and I think that is why *Scholarship Reconsidered* really moved ahead" (personal communication, April 15, 2014). Boyer began with Rice's manuscript, added survey data of more than five thousand faculty members, made considerable revisions, and placed a new title on the project: *Scholarship Reconsidered: Priorities of the Professoriate.* One name was then placed in the author's line—Ernest L. Boyer, President, Carnegie Foundation for the Advancement of Teaching.

Boyer and his team at the foundation spent much of 1989 surveying, collecting, and analyzing data from the more than five thousand faculty members from all types of higher education institutions.[11] The survey asked questions related to teaching, research, tenure, and professional satisfaction. The results were stunning—over 70 percent of the faculty reported a strong interest in teaching, many of whom advocated that teaching be a primary criterion for promotion.[12] Charles Glassick, another Carnegie Foundation senior fellow, concluded, "Clearly, the majority of faculty considered teaching to be a central mission and enjoyed the time they spent with students."[13]

These results revealed the dissonance between what faculty members valued and what they were rewarded for accomplishing. The majority of faculty members desired to teach and spend time interacting with students. The dominant reward structure of the modern university recognized faculty members who could successfully distance themselves from the classroom so that they could spend more time on research. However, the quality of that research was difficult to determine.

More than a third of the faculty respondents reported their institutions simply counted publications regardless of their quality.[14] Even at research universities, 42 percent agreed a systemic lack of quality control in scholarship existed. Boyer's speeches and writings on scholarship thus proposed a broader vision of scholarship.

The nuance may initially seem slight, but it nonetheless proved profound. The focal point of Ernest Boyer's work was not necessarily the scholar but the student. Peer review played a role in scholarship but was merely a means to the end of a Boyerian approach—effective communication to students. In other words, Boyer viewed scholarship as a highly communal act. In a speech to the American Academy of Arts and Sciences, he explained:

> You never get tenured for research alone. You get tenured for research and publication, which means you have to teach somebody what you've learned. And academics must continue to communicate, not only with their peers, but also with future scholars in the classroom in order to keep the flame of scholarship alive.[15]

A communal act for the sake of student learning was not the traditional milieu of American scholarship. However, for Boyer, whose writings and speeches reveal a convergence of his key philosophical tenets of education (connectedness, service, language, and teaching), it proved to be a logical extension. If these attributes are the building blocks of a quality education, they must have an impact on scholarship within collegiate education. A Boyerian view of scholarship requires a connection to a community. Scholarship for scholarship's sake is wasteful. It must serve the common good, and this commitment was the essence of his call for an education of coherence.[16]

As a result, Boyer's most popular work, *Scholarship Reconsidered*, was written and released to the American public. He wanted to shift the paradigm of scholarship to value qualities universities had lost: community, service, and teaching. He thus proposed a view of scholarship that included four domains: application, discovery, integration, and teaching.

He sent a pre-publication manuscript of the report to an anonymous, yet reportedly distinguished, Princeton historian to garner feedback. Boyer included a note in the manuscript with the following disclaimer: "I don't think you'll like it very much, but please give it a read." The historian responded, "You're right! I don't like it very much."[17] Ernest also sent a copy to his brother Paul, another distinguished American historian at the University of Wisconsin, Madison. Paul's response was similar, albeit a bit more sympathetic.

Boyer accepted the critique yet remained convinced that scholarship could prove excellent and accessible—the mantra of his tenure as US Commissioner of Education and the Carnegie Foundation. If education can pursue both excellence and access, then scholarship should as well. The initial response to *Scholarship Reconsidered* was a foretaste of what was to come. It became Boyer's most influential work because, in many ways, it also proved to be his most controversial. Glenn R. Bucher and Jennell

J. Patton provide a helpful response through which to explore Boyer's view of scholarship:

> To understand *Scholarship Reconsidered* ... is to see it as moving the notion of service into the center of the academic enterprise. [Boyer] proposed the scholarships of application, discovery, integration, and teaching partly as a critique of more elitist notions of university research. Then he offered the scholarship of engagement as an encompassing category, one that continues to require further development.[18]

The report quickly became a Carnegie Foundation best-seller yet, according to Charles E. Glassick, *Scholarship Reconsidered* "clearly had struck a nerve in higher education."[19] The response was mixed and passionate. Regardless of whether scholars loved or loathed his four domains, Ernest Boyer provided a much-desired vocabulary for a national debate on the issue of scholarship. In Glassick's estimation, "*Scholarship Reconsidered* lacked specificity, [but] its concepts ... were immediately recognized as important new proposals in a field that was ripe for revision."[20]

The majority of responses to Boyer's views of scholarship were positive. Many praised *Scholarship Reconsidered* for expanding the thinking of the academy to a broader definition of scholarship.[21] Others also praised Boyer for not just challenging the reigning definition of scholarship but also fostering comprehensive reform to higher education. One group of scholars wrote:

> A broadened view of scholarship that is congruent with progressive missions invites changes in the academic culture that touch faculty roles, reward systems, disciplinary boundaries, and changing purposes. ... Learning becomes the measure of success rather than teaching—a challenging but worthy endeavor.[22]

Stephen G. Estes may have summed it up best when he wrote that "Boyer's approach to scholarship is *scholarly*. ... Boyer was a scholar of scholarship."[23]

Scholars and administrators welcomed the four domains as a breath of fresh air. Others liked portions of Boyer's view, accepting some while critiquing others. Michael Paulsen and Kenneth Feldman mostly praised Boyer's efforts, but they suggested replacing the scholarship of integration with their own "scholarship of academic citizenship."[24]

A large number of scholars were critical of Boyer's entire framework. Alexander McNeil proved one of the strongest critics. In particular, he admitted that Boyer's intention to broaden scholarship was noble, conceding that the report raised the collective consciousness surrounding scholarship in higher education. However, he strongly critiqued Boyer's scholarship of teaching: "Boyer's intention is to broaden our concept of scholarship within the university. But he has succeeded only in clouding the issue. Part of the cloudiness results from his failure to draw a relationship between teaching and learning."[25] Alan Rubin was also not impressed, claiming that Boyer's view of scholarship only succeeded in leading to a "scholarship of confusion."[26] His primary concern was that Boyer was dangerously inclusive. Should everything an academic does be defined as scholarship? If so, does this not diminish the quality of scholarship? Rubin believed "it fosters the potential for superficial work, isolation and division, and the lack of common or shared values."[27]

Clearly, Boyer's view of scholarship was controversial in higher education. Glassick then summarized the tension well, explaining that an expanded definition of scholarship was generally well received, but two main areas provided stumbling blocks.[28] First, what is the meaning of the scholarship of teaching? Second, how should the quality of scholarship be assessed?

Regardless of one's view of teaching's scholarly validity, Boyer achieved what he set out to do with all of his reports—he started a conversation that elevated teaching from the fringes of higher education to the center. Rarely in Boyer's career did he intend to provide definitive answers; rather, he was more comfortable providing the framework for a vibrant discussion. For individuals who found great joy in the act of teaching at the university level, Boyer provided legitimacy. For individuals who focused solely on traditional research and publication, Boyer provided a challenge.

Boyer's view of scholarship served as a catalyst for conversation on the nature and purpose of higher education in the United States and his work is still relevant today. It endures as part of the national conversation on higher education.[29] On one level, it continues to be a prominent text in the canon of higher education literature. On a more critical level, it serves as a powerful point of convergence of Boyer's experience and theology. It weaves his love for the diversity of higher education and his vision for university renewal. This vision for renewal flowed out of a deep call to service where he sought the connectedness of all things expressed through language.

This connected expression of learning was then placed in the context of a community that served one another. Scholarship is a prime example of Boyer's ability to go beneath the surface of an issue. When many saw the need to change tenure or promotion policies and procedures, Boyer saw a broken community that had lost touch with its roots. The state of scholarship in the academy was merely the symptom of a larger problem. In essence, the professoriate had lost its connectivity to one another, its students, and to the wider public.

In *Scholarship Reconsidered*, Boyer accomplished what most others were unable to do: provide a new lens through which to consider the work of the academy. He alone was uniquely positioned for this role, because his story differed from any common trajectory of higher education leaders. It is these lesser known parts of his story that shaped this framework for scholarship. Boyer's background consists of a childhood at the side of his preaching grandfather; a humble academic background in small, faith-based liberal arts colleges; a charismatic public persona; and a capacity to leverage his stature by surrounding himself with key people to carry out his agenda. Boyer's life was lived through a unique lens, one he shared with the academy. This uniqueness is likely why his views are sometimes critiqued for being impractical or vague. Yet, in the twenty-five years since *Scholarship Reconsidered*'s release, we still wait for someone to publish anything that comes close to Boyer's persisting, central place in conversations about scholarship in the academy.

BOYER'S IMPACT ON FACULTY DEVELOPMENT

Andrea L. Beach

"The work of the professor becomes consequential only as it is understood by others."[1] With this simple statement, Ernest Boyer introduced ideas that would develop into perhaps the most recognizable and widespread of the scholarships he advocated—the Scholarship of Teaching and Learning. The impact that *Scholarship Reconsidered* has had on academe is all the more impressive when one considers how brief the section of that report is that lays out his vision of teaching as a scholarly pursuit. With a length of seven paragraphs, Boyer made a case that a scholarship of teaching be aligned with the scholarships of integration and application and equal in importance to the scholarship of discovery, which was most familiar to and understood by those in academe. He focused primarily on scholarly teaching and argued that engaged teaching is an enticement to scholarship and a link between the other scholarships and student learning. Boyer's colleagues at the Carnegie Foundation for the Advancement of Teaching offered two decades of further refinement of the concept of the scholarship of teaching and learning (SoTL), its distinction from excellent (or scholarly) teaching,[2] culminating in Hutchings, Huber, and Ciccone's discussion of its growth and impact in *Scholarship of Teaching and Learning Reconsidered.*[3] In twenty-five years, SoTL has gone from an idea to an international movement and in many ways has shaped the field of faculty development during that same time period.

This chapter will offer some historical perspective on faculty development as a field and its connection with Boyer's work, discuss ways in which SoTL is currently contributing to faculty development, provide some data on the spread of SoTL as a focus of faculty development in both the United States and abroad, and consider future directions given the recent interest in undergraduate instruction, particularly in science, technology, engineering, and mathematics (STEM).

At the time Boyer published *Scholarship Reconsidered,* the field of faculty development was still in its very early stages. The Professional and Organizational Development (POD) Network, the scholarly and professional association of faculty and educational developers, was barely fifteen years old. It was established in 1976 as an outgrowth of the American Association of Higher Education (AAHE) in response to what its founding coordinator, Joan North, called an "explosion" of committees, offices, positions, and projects in the early 1970s devoted to institutional renewal through what came to be known as "faculty development."[4] By 1990, the quotation marks were removed but questions of how and to what end faculty development professionals engaged with their colleagues remained. The POD Network's early members and core committee developed clear values, an ethical code, and guidelines for practice to clearly delineate the consultative and developmental nature of the field.

By 1990, faculty development was emerging from a decade of rapid expansion. Sorcinelli, Austin, Eddy, and Beach identified that time period (the 1980s) as the "Age of the Developer," when the profession "came of age" and began to define itself.[5] Scholars in higher education had increasingly focused on improvement and evaluation of teaching in the 1970s. In the 1980s, that research was put into practice, fueled by national reports urging more attention to undergraduate education.[6] Boyer's own voice was prominent in this discussion.[7] The 1990s ushered in a focus on teaching as the *facilitation of student learning* rather than as an act unto itself separated from its outcomes. Sorcinelli and colleagues called it the "Age of the Learner."[8] As a field, faculty development was central to the growth in this new focus on learners and learning, and the developing SoTL concepts and practices, discussed by Mary Taylor Huber in the foreword of this book, were significant to the growth of faculty development.

To think of teaching as scholarly was a radical notion when Boyer proposed it, as was the idea of academic biologists, historians, economists, and physicians engaging in research on their students' learning outcomes in response to planned changes in their own instructional practices. They did not see teaching as something that, in its wider shared understanding, made their work consequential. SoTL offered faculty development professionals a set of ideas, practices, and a language with which they could engage faculty members who placed teaching and learning on a level more equal to traditional conceptions of scholarship and research. It was a language they could understand. SoTL also provided a new focus for faculty development programs—helping faculty members engage in SoTL research as a process of professional development and as an opportunity for presentation and publication. Hutchings and colleagues called it a transformative concept in higher education.[9]

Individual consultation has always served as bedrock of faculty development practice. Many centers for teaching and learning were built on consultation, observation, and feedback in response to the needs of individual faculty members and still see those tools as a central tool to fostering change. SoTL offers another approach to instructional change—one that compels faculty members to ask and answer questions they may have always had about their students' learning but had little context within which to follow through. In addition, it requires that faculty members share their thinking about teaching, lifting teaching out of the realm of the routine and into a shared communal space. This is the essence of what Boyer believed made teaching scholarly.

At the same time that SoTL practices and standards, conferences, and journals were being developed, a new approach to faculty development—faculty learning communities (FLCs)—was emerging. The two have been linked ever since, and it is difficult for me as a faculty developer to think about SoTL without also thinking about its relationship to and contribution to FLCs. Shortly after *Scholarship Reconsidered* introduced the concepts of scholarly teaching and SoTL, the first work appeared describing FLCs as structures within which to support faculty engagement in SoTL.[10] To underscore how new both of these practices were to faculty development at the time, Cox later noted that neither was mentioned in a 1994 international survey of teaching improvement practices.[11] Those circumstances quickly changed. Cox and his colleagues went on to provide extensive literature on the structures, processes, and outcomes of FLCs based on the model developed at Miami University.[12] Richlin and Essington reported the results of a 2003 national survey seeking out FLCs and identified 308 FLCs at 132 institutions.[13] The most prevalent topic of the FLCs reported was SoTL.

In 2009, Beach and Cox reported results of outcomes from an initiative to develop FLC programs at six universities based on the Miami model.[14] They found participants' top self-reported outcomes centered on their increased appreciation for teaching and learning outside their disciplines, interest in the teaching process, understanding of and interest in SoTL, and view of teaching and learning as an intellectual pursuit. All these outcomes directly relate to the kinds of thinking about teaching and learning that fit Boyer's description of the university as a community.[15]

What other evidence puts the growing importance of SoTL to faculty development into context? In 2001, Sorcinelli, Austin, Eddy, and Beach surveyed the POD membership to explore the priorities and practices of the field. SoTL was identified in the top ten services that faculty development professionals saw as important to offer and also reported offering.[16] Perhaps counterintuitively, research and comprehensive universities reported a higher interest and engagement in SoTL than liberal arts colleges or community colleges.

In 2012, the survey was repeated with slightly different questions.[17] SoTL is now among the top five services related to teaching and learning and remains in the top ten of all services offered by faculty development professionals. It is also in the top ten "signature" programs offered—those that respondents felt were their best or best known. Further, faculty development professionals were asked what they would add to their portfolio of offerings, given more resources. SoTL topped the responses for research and comprehensive university development professionals and was second overall in all responses.

In addition to survey results highlighting the growing role of SoTL in faculty development (and vice versa), a simple Google search brings into focus the number of conference presentations and workshops, journals, and books dedicated to the practice and results of SoTL, many offered and authored by faculty development professionals (and too numerous to cite). SoTL even has its own Wikipedia page (www.en.wikipedia.org/wiki/scholarship_of_teaching_and_learning).

The results of all the development efforts and research emerging from the United States would extend across numerous other countries because both faculty development and SoTL are now globally practiced and connected. The International Consortium of Educational Developers (ICED) is a network of scholarly associations of faculty and education development professionals that draws its members from the national associations of multiple countries. The International Society for the Scholarship of Teaching and Learning (ISSoTL) connects SoTL researchers from across the globe. Both offer scholarly journals with international scope and join the growing number of nationally focused journals of educational development and SoTL.

Looking to the future, trends in higher education present important opportunities and imperatives for faculty development and for new SoTL work. Two that are most urgent are the increasing diversity of college students and the increasing focus on improving undergraduate STEM education. A highly heterogeneous student population is the new normal in American colleges and universities. Students with learning disabilities, from underperforming high schools, who are first-generation college students, who are adults returning from active military duty, and who come from widely varied national and international backgrounds form a large and growing percentage of our student bodies. As a result, we cannot simply assume that the practices recommended and outcomes achieved even ten years ago are still relevant today or for the future. SoTL that is focused on the different needs and outcomes of diverse groups of students is critical to supporting student success.

Because SoTL focuses on teaching and learning as it unfolds, it can provide authentic assessment of practice and outcomes to complement more traditional approaches to studying student learning. In addition diverse students make up a large and growing percentage of community college enrollments. Encouraging SoTL in the community college classroom is therefore critical. Large community colleges may have centers for teaching and learning that can support faculty engagement in SoTL, but many smaller colleges do not. Survey data from 2001 and 2012 indicate that SoTL is not as high a priority for community college faculty development professionals as it is for those in research and comprehensive universities.[18] How can bridges be built to ensure that we are studying our students' learning in all of its contexts? Educational development and SoTL associations can play a leadership role in expanding partnerships among community colleges and universities to support inter-institutional SoTL.

The growing interest and investment in improvement of undergraduate STEM education is driven by the national need for a stronger and more diverse STEM workforce. In response, several highly visible initiatives have adopted or adapted SoTL as part of improvement processes. For example, the Center for the Integration of Research, Teaching, and Learning and its network of research universities is committed to infusing graduate programs in the sciences with both pedagogical education and the concept of teaching as research, an adaptation of SoTL by instructors to apply scientific research skills and ways of knowing to investigate and measure student learning.[19]

The rise of discipline-based educational research in STEM fields has given legitimacy to the examination of student learning and instructional best practices (evidence-based practice). The American Association of Universities' STEM Initiative, the Bayview Alliance, and National Science Foundation WIDER projects all focus on improvement of undergraduate learning, involve groups of faculty members working together to transform undergraduate courses, and are national in their scope. Results from their work can provide theoretically grounded and empirically tested approaches for other STEM faculty members to apply and study in their own SoTL work.

One practice of which I have not seen much evidence and which will prove crucial for the continued scholarly reputation and usefulness of SoTL is the integration and application of SoTL results into new SoTL projects—the replication and expansion of SoTL. Recent writing on SoTL practice includes discussions of the need to ground new work in prior SoTL results.[20] Faculty development professionals can help faculty members access, interpret, and apply the SoTL literature—perhaps from very different disciplines—as they plan their own projects.

The POD Network turns forty in 2015. Where will the next twenty-five years of Boyer's seminal work take the field of faculty development? Beach and colleagues identified the current period as the "Age of Evidence" for faculty development and indeed for higher education.[21] The national and international calls for evidence-based instructional practice, for accountability in undergraduate education, and for evidence of impact of faculty development programs are loud and urgent. The field has a responsibility to help faculty members understand how they can research their teaching, individually and collectively, within the context of their own disciplines and across disciplinary boundaries. Faculty developers will need to be champions and leaders of conversations about institutional supports and barriers to faculty engagement in SoTL. We will also need to expand our role in propagating high-quality SoTL research that builds not only on faculty member interests in their own questions but also on the vast education research and SoTL literature.

To sum up Ernest Boyer's impact on faculty development, it is safe to say that without his call to treat teaching as a scholarly enterprise and all of the work it sparked, the field would not have as rich a source of ideas and practices with which to engage faculty members in their own development and improvement. The past twenty-five years have seen vibrant growth for faculty development and SoTL, and have positioned both, together, for an equally vibrant future.

THE INFLUENCE OF *SCHOLARSHIP RECONSIDERED* ON INSTITUTIONAL TYPES AND ACADEMIC DISCIPLINES

John M. Braxton

In addition to teaching, research constitutes one of the core activities of college and university faculty members.[1] Faculty member research performance varies across the structural dimension of institutional type[2] and academic discipline.[3] Types of colleges and universities range from teaching-oriented colleges and universities (e.g., comprehensive colleges and universities, liberal arts colleges, and community colleges) to research-oriented universities (research universities and doctorate-granting universities). Faculty publication productivity varies across these types of colleges and universities.[4]

Academic disciplines constitute the second structural dimension that demarcates differences among college and university faculty members. Faculty research performance also varies across this structural dimension. Braxton and Hargens concluded from their review of research on discipline differences that the dissimilarities between academic disciplines are "profound and extensive." Such differences include publication rates and orientations toward research.[5]

In *Scholarship Reconsidered: Priorities of the Profession,* Ernest L. Boyer put forth three assertions that have implications for the research role of college and university faculty members in different types of colleges and universities and in different academic disciplines. First, Boyer asserted that the definition of scholarship should be expanded beyond discovery to include the scholarship of application, integration, and teaching. The second key assertion made by Boyer concerns the need for the type of scholarship stressed by colleges and universities to align with their missions. Boyer provides prescriptions for the domain of scholarship or rather domain of scholarship that particular types of colleges and universities should stress.[6]

In addition to these two assertions, Boyer also contended that types of scholarly outcomes distinct from publications (journal articles, book chapters, and books) should also be used to assess faculty research performance.[7] For a scholarly outcome distinct from publications to be designated as scholarship, it must meet three necessary criteria: it must be public, it must be amenable to critical appraisal, and it must be in a form that enables its use by other members of the scholarly community.[8] Braxton, Luckey, and Helland refer to such outcomes as unpublished, but publicly observable, outcomes.[9]

Looking now at the twenty-fifth anniversary of *Scholarship Reconsidered*, these three assertions give rise to the following questions that I address using existing literature and research finding:

- Do college and university faculty members' levels of engagement in Boyer's four domains of scholarship vary across different types of colleges and universities and across different academic disciplines?
- Do such levels of engagement vary when scholarship is measured using publications as well as unpublished, but publicly observable, outcomes?
- Do college and university faculty members' levels of engagement in each of the four domains of scholarship correspond to Boyer's prescriptions for institutional domains emphasis? Do such levels of engagement vary when scholarship is measured using publications as well as unpublished, but publicly observable, outcomes?

I address the first two questions and then organize the findings derived from previous research by each of the four domains of scholarship. I do not describe the goals of each of these domains, however, because they have been described in previous chapters.

Among four-year colleges and universities, faculty members holding academic appointments in research and doctorate-granting universities produced a greater number of publications within a three-year time period reflective of the scholarship of application than faculty members in comprehensive colleges and universities and liberal arts colleges of both higher and lower undergraduate admissions selectivity. However, these institutional differences fade when using unpublished, but publicly observable, outcomes of scholarship pertinent to this scholarship domain as an indicator of faculty engagement in the scholarship of application. Examples of such outcomes include conducting a study for a local organization and conducting a study to help solve a community problem.[10] More specifically, faculty members in research universities, doctorate-granting universities, comprehensive colleges and universities, and liberal arts colleges (higher and lower undergraduate admissions selectivity) produce similar levels of such unpublished, but publicly observable, outcomes.

Although lacking comparisons among different types of community colleges, recent research on community college faculty engagement in the scholarship of application provides some indication of the extent of engagement in this particular domain of scholarship. The vast majority (87.4 percent) in a national sample of community college faculty members report no publications within a three-year period of time that reflect the scholarship of application. However, three-fourths (75.2 percent) of such community college faculty members report some unpublished, but publicly observable, outcomes of scholarship pertinent to this domain of scholarship.[11]

Among faculty members in four-year colleges and universities, those in chemistry generate more publications within a three-year period related to the scholarship of application than do their colleagues in the academic disciplines of biology and history. When using unpublished, but publicly observable, outcomes of scholarship reflective of this domain, a different pattern of discipline emerges, with academic sociologists producing more such outcomes than faculty members in chemistry and history.[12]

Discipline differences among faculty members in community colleges also spring forth. Those who are sociologists publish more within this domain of scholarship than do community college faculty members who are biologists or historians. However, those who are historians generate more unpublished, but publicly observable, outcomes of scholarship within this domain than faculty members in community colleges who are chemists.[13]

At this juncture, I found no studies reporting the levels of performance of unpublished, but publicly observable, forms of the outcomes of scholarship reflective of the scholarship of discovery in the literature. As a consequence, I describe in the following only levels of publications pertinent to this domain of scholarship.

Faculty members in research universities produce more publications within a three-year period pertinent to the scholarship of discovery than those in the doctorate-granting universities, comprehensive colleges and universities, and liberal arts colleges of both higher and lower admissions selectivity.[14] Similar to their levels of publication related to the scholarship of application, the vast proportion (80.6 percent) of full-time community college faculty members have not published within a three-year period of time any scholarship reflective of the scholarship of discovery. Nevertheless, less than one-fifth (19.4 percent) of community college faculty members report some publications within this domain of scholarship during the past three years.[15]

In four-year colleges and universities faculty members in the disciplines of biology, chemistry, history, and sociology produce similar levels of publications related to the scholarship of discovery.[16] A similar pattern of publication productivity within the scholarship of discovery also pertains to community college faculty members in these same four academic disciplines.[17]

Similar to the scholarship of application, faculty members in research and doctorate-granting universities generate more publications within a three-year time frame germane to the scholarship of integration than those holding academic appointments in comprehensive colleges and universities and in liberal arts colleges of both higher and lower admissions selectivity. However, faculty members across these types of four-year colleges and universities display similar levels of production of unpublished, but publicly observable, outcomes of scholarship reflective of the scholarship of integration. Examples of such outcomes include a lecture on a current disciplinary topic given at a local community college and a talk on a current disciplinary topic on a local radio station.[18]

Although the majority (55.3 percent) of full-time faculty members in community colleges have not published any scholarship related to the scholarship of integration with the past three years, a little more than two-fifths (44.7 percent) of such community college faculty members report some publications within this domain of scholarship. Moreover, nearly two-thirds (61.2 percent) of community college faculty members holding full-time status report produced some unpublished, but publicly observable, outcomes of scholarship reflective of the scholarship of integration.[19]

Within the ranks of faculty members holding appointments in four-year colleges and universities, academic historians produce a higher level of publications pertinent to the scholarship of integration than their counterparts in the disciplines of biology, chemistry, and sociology. Moreover, academic sociologists also generate more publications within this domain of scholarship than do those in the disciplines of biology and chemistry.[20] These publication levels occurred within a three-year period of time.

Using unpublished, but publicly observable, outcomes of scholarship as an indicator of engagement in the scholarship of integration domain, academic sociologists and historians in four-year colleges and universities also outpace those in the disciplines of biology and chemistry in their production of this outcome of scholarship as they do in the production of publications reflective of the scholarship of integration.[21]

Similar to sociologists in four-year colleges and universities, academic sociologists in community colleges also generate more publications reflective of the scholarship of integration than chemists holding full-time appointments in community colleges. Moreover, similar to their disciplinary colleagues in four-year colleges and universities, academic sociologists and historians in community colleges also outperform faculty members in the disciplines of biology and chemistry in their production of unpublished, but publicly observable, outcomes of scholarship indicative of the scholarship of integration.[22]

Faculty members in research universities, doctorate-granting universities, comprehensive colleges and universities, and liberal arts colleges generate a similar level of publication reflective of the scholarship of teaching within a three-year frame of time.[23] However, some institutional differences occur when unpublished, but publicly observable, outcomes of scholarship reflective of the scholarship of teaching are used to assess faculty engagement in the scholarship of teaching. More specifically, faculty members in liberal arts (both higher and lower admissions selectivity) colleges produce more of these forms of scholarship than those in research universities.[24] Examples of such outcomes include presentations about new instructional techniques to colleagues and the creation of an approach or strategy to help students to think critically about course concepts.

When using publications as a determining factor of engagement, full-time community college faculty members show little involvement in the scholarship of teaching given that the vast majority (86.2 percent) report no publications during the past three years. In stark contrast, almost all full-time (99.4 percent) faculty members in community colleges report varying numbers of unpublished, but publicly observable, outcomes of scholarship reflective of the scholarship of teaching during the past three years.[25]

Faculty members in four-year colleges and universities[26] and in community colleges[27] report little or no engagement in the scholarship of teaching. This assertion remains constant when both publications and unpublished, but publicly observable, outcomes of scholarship reflective of the scholarship of teaching are used as indicators of faculty member involvement in this domain of scholarship.[28] As previously stated, Boyer contended that the type of scholarship stressed by colleges and universities needs to align with their missions.[29] In making this argument, he provided prescriptions for the domain of scholarship or rather domains of scholarship that particular types of colleges and universities should stress. More specifically he offered such prescriptions for research universities, doctorate-granting universities, comprehensive colleges and universities, liberal arts colleges, and community colleges.[30]

In making these recommendations, Boyer sought to align the type of scholarship emphasized with the missions of these five types of colleges and universities. These recommendations follow. I also present the findings of research conducted using faculty members in each of these five types of colleges and universities addressing this question: To what extent do faculty members in these five types of colleges and universities follow Boyer's prescriptions for domain emphasis?

Boyer asserted that an institutional emphasis on the scholarship of discovery should prevail in research universities.[31] However, he posited that the scholarship of application, integration, and teaching should also receive some attention.[32]

This prescription receives support among faculty members in research universities given that academics in this institutional setting publish more scholarship pertinent to the scholarship of discovery than those in doctorate-granting universities, comprehensive colleges and universities, and liberal arts colleges. Moreover, faculty members in research universities also publish more within the domain of the scholarship of discovery than they do scholarship oriented toward application, integration, and teaching.[33]

Although Boyer posited that the scholarship of discovery should receive some attention in doctorate-granting universities, he asserted that the scholarship of application, integration, and teaching should receive particular emphasis.[34] As Boyer suggests, faculty members in doctorate-granting universities do give some attention to the scholarship of discovery given that they publish more scholarship directed toward discovery than they do scholarship oriented toward application, integration, and teaching.[35]

Although faculty members in doctorate-granting universities publish more discovery-focused scholarship than scholarship reflective of the other three domains, they also produce more publications reflective of the scholarship of application than those in comprehensive colleges and universities and in liberal arts colleges.[36] However, their generation of such publications resembles the level of faculty members in research universities for this particular scholarship domain.

Although faculty members in doctorate-granting universities publish some pieces related to the scholarship of integration and teaching, their levels of publication productivity in these two domains do not surpass their engagement in the scholarship of application.[37] This configuration of findings suggests that faculty in doctorate-granting universities meet Boyer's prescriptions for institutional domain emphasis for the scholarship of application and discovery.

A redefinition of the form of scholarship emphasized in comprehensive colleges and universities seems most fitting according to Boyer.[38] Accordingly, he asserted that as a type of institution, comprehensive colleges and universities should embrace the scholarship of application, integration, and teaching. However, individual comprehensive colleges and universities may choose to stress any of these three domains of scholarship.

Evidence suggests that faculty members in comprehensive colleges and universities favor engagement in the scholarship of application over the scholarship of teaching, given that they tend to publish more application-oriented scholarship than scholarship reflective of teaching. They produce similar levels of publications reflective of the scholarship domains of application and integration. However, they publish the most in the scholarship of discovery than in the three other domains.[39] When using unpublished, but publicly observable, outcomes of scholarship reflective of the scholarship of teaching as an index of engagement in this domain, faculty members in compressive colleges and universities produce more of this form of teaching-focused scholarship than application or integration.

This configuration of findings suggests that faculty members in comprehensive colleges and universities follow Boyer's prescriptions regarding the choice of the scholarship of application, the scholarship of integration, and the scholarship of teaching. Nevertheless, as indicated, faculty members in this type of institution of higher learning publish more scholarship centered on discovery than the three other domains of scholarship.

Boyer posited that the scholarship of teaching should receive primary emphasis in liberal arts colleges. Moreover, Boyer also viewed the scholarship of integration as befitting because of the "climate of intellectual exchange that fosters interdisciplinary studies, creative general education courses, and capstone seminars" found at liberal arts colleges.[40]

Although faculty members in liberal arts colleges of both higher and lower admissions selectivity publish to a limited degree scholarship reflective of the domains of integration and teaching, they publish more discovery-oriented scholarship than these two domains prescribed by Boyer for liberal arts colleges. The use of unpublished, but publicly observable, outcomes of scholarship as an indicator of faculty member engagement provides a different picture. Faculty members in both types of liberal arts colleges produce more of this form of scholarship related to the scholarship of teaching domain than the scholarship of integration. Thus, faculty members in liberal arts colleges follow Boyer's prescriptions for the scholarship of teaching more than for the scholarship of integration.

Because teaching constitutes the predominate mission of community colleges, Boyer suggested that the scholarship of teaching should receive some attention in this type of institution of higher education.[41] Because many community college students enroll in technical and career programs, Boyer viewed the scholarship of application as a suitable emphasis for individuals serving in these institutions.[42] He also suggested that the scholarship of integration might also receive some attention.

Full-time faculty members in community colleges follow all three of Boyer's prescriptions for institutional domain emphasis. In terms of publications, individual faculty members in community colleges meet Boyer's recommendation for emphasis on the scholarship of integration. As previously stated, about two-fifths (44.7 percent) of community college faculty members report some publications within this domain of scholarship. However, the vast majority of them report no publications associated with the scholarship of teaching and the scholarship of application during the past three years.[43]

Moreover, the use of unpublished, but publicly observable, outcomes of scholarship as an indicator of faculty engagement enabled me to regard as fulfilled Boyer's prescriptions for institutional domain emphasis on the scholarship of application and teaching. More specifically, the vast majority of full-time community college faculty members report some unpublished, but publicly observable, outcomes of scholarship pertinent to the scholarship of application and the scholarship of teaching.

I offer three conclusions that each correspond to Boyer's three assertions regarding scholarship that he made in *Scholarship Reconsidered.*[44] First, Boyer posited that the definition of scholarship should be broadened beyond the scholarship of discovery to include the scholarships of application, integration, and teaching. The research findings I reviewed suggest a conclusion that these domains of scholarship differentiate college and university faculty members by their institutional affiliation and by their academic discipline. To elaborate, the existing pattern of institutional differences in general publication productivity reproduces itself when publications are differentiated by the domain of reflected scholarship. The existing pattern of general publication productivity takes the following form: faculty members in research and doctoral-granting universities generate higher levels of publications than do faculty members in teaching-oriented colleges and universities.[45]

The research findings I reviewed indicate that this same pattern of institutional ordering takes place because faculty members in research and doctorate-granting universities produce more publications in the scholarship domains of application, discovery, and integration than those in comprehensive colleges and universities, liberal arts colleges of higher and lower admissions selectivity, and community colleges. However, no such institutional differences pertain to publications of the scholarship of teaching. Thus, faculty member engagement in the scholarships of application, discovery, and integration function as a source of differentiation among college and university faculty members in different types of colleges and universities ranging from research universities to community colleges.

Moreover, my review of research findings regarding discipline differences in publication productivity in each of the four domains of scholarship reinforces the conclusion offered by Braxton and Hargens that the differences among academic disciplines are "profound and extensive"[46] Although no differences across disciplines transpire for the scholarship of discovery and teaching, differences can be found in the scholarship of application and integration. As a consequence, faculty member engagement in these two domains of scholarship functions as a further source of differentiation among faculty members in different academic disciplines because of a pure orientation toward their subject matter. The four academic disciplines discussed in this chapter—biology, chemistry, history, and sociology—are classified as having a pure orientation according to Biglan's schema for the classification of academic disciplines.[47]

Second, the traditional template used to assess faculty member scholarship role performance includes the use of books, book chapters, and articles in refereed academic journals.[48] The use of this template greatly misrepresents the extent of individual college and university faculty member's engagement in scholarship performance especially in comprehensive colleges and universities, liberal arts colleges, and community colleges.

When using such indictors as unpublished, but publicly observable, outcomes of scholarship, I learned faculty members in teaching-oriented two- and four-year colleges and universities demonstrate some degree of engagement in scholarship. More specifically, faculty members in research and doctorate-granting universities publish more scholarship reflective of the domains of application and integration than do those in teaching-oriented two- and four-year colleges and universities. However, these differences dwindle when we use unpublished, but publicly observable, outcomes of scholarship oriented toward these two domains as indicators of domain engagement. Moreover, the use of publications greatly underestimates the degree of community college faculty member engagement in the scholarship of teaching. These formulations provide robust support for Boyer's assertion that types of scholarly outcomes distinct from publications (journal articles, book chapters, and books) should also be used to assess faculty member research performance.

Third, because of the predominate value placed on the scholarship of discovery, Boyer asserted that the type of scholarship generated by faculty members fails to align with the missions of all but the research university. Accordingly, Boyer formulated prescriptions for institutional domain emphasis that serve to align the scholarship stressed with the mission of different types of colleges and universities. With the exception of liberal arts colleges, individual faculty members in research universities, doctorate-granting universities, comprehensive colleges and universities, and community colleges engage in scholarship congruent with Boyer's prescriptions. Nevertheless, some misalignment still persists given that faculty members in comprehensive colleges and universities and in liberal arts colleges publish more scholarship reflective of the scholarship of discovery than the other three domains.

Without establishing causation, the three conclusions advanced suggest that the key assertions made by Boyer in *Scholarship Reconsidered* wield a substantial influence on different of types of institutions of higher education and on different academic disciplines. The greatest influence pertains to the scholarship of teaching in liberal arts colleges—higher and lower admissions selectivity—and in community colleges. For Boyer's influence to be greatest in liberal arts colleges and community colleges speaks volumes about the efficacy of his call for the alignment of institutional missions and the type of scholarship stressed. In the case of liberal arts colleges and community colleges, an emphasis on the scholarship of teaching aligns with the teaching-oriented mission of these two types of institutions of higher education.

In closing, these conclusions speak volumes about the legacy of Boyer's *Scholarship Reconsidered* to higher education. In addition to his delineation and description of the four domains of scholarship, his legacy finds expression in a movement toward a better alignment between the missions of colleges and universities and their reward structures as well as his assertion that types of scholarly outcomes distinct from publications should also be used to assess faculty member research performance.[49] Such a legacy should endure beyond the twenty-five years of the anniversary of the publication of *Scholarship Reconsidered: Priorities of the Profession.*

SCHOLARSHIP RECONSIDERED'S IMPACT ON DOCTORAL AND PROFESSIONAL EDUCATION

Ann E. Austin and Melissa McDaniels

Ernest L. Boyer wrote *Scholarship Reconsidered* at the beginning of an era of great flux in a number of economic sectors and thus also in a number of professions in the United States. His work provided a conceptual anchor and a call to action for graduate and professional education—propelling graduate faculty members, administrators, policy makers, and other members of the professions to think about and identify core elements of scholarship and the implications of the definition of scholarship for individuals working in academic and professional areas. This chapter begins by exploring factors affecting how and what graduate students preparing for careers as postsecondary faculty members, lawyers, doctors, and other professionals are learning in their graduate programs and then analyzes ways in which *Scholarship Reconsidered* has particular relevance for doctoral and professional education.

Trends across a variety of economic sectors have had a significant impact on the structure, content, and processes of doctoral and professional education in the United States. In particular, we will highlight three trends that stand out in terms of their implications for doctoral and professional education and the ways in which they relate to the impact of Boyer's work.

First, the nature of employment opportunities for graduates of doctoral and professional programs has been changing. For aspiring faculty members, the labor market for traditional faculty positions has been far smaller than the pool of scholars prepared with advanced degrees. A notable shift from tenure-track positions to non-tenure-track positions has been evident, as has a growing proportion of part-time positions.[1] Accompanying this shift is often an unbundling of faculty member work, through which their positions may require scholars to emphasize particular dimensions of scholarly work, such as teaching or curriculum development.

In the medical profession, aspiring physicians are increasingly being employed in health management organizations rather than establishing themselves as independent health care providers. Clinical faculty members responsible for teaching future physicians are having less time to teach, and hospitals within which future physicians are trained are either unable or unwilling to support the teaching mission.[2] Students being trained for the legal profession are also facing employment in a sector that looks very different than it did decades ago. According to a recent American Bar Association report, the rapid pace of structural changes includes the increased use of contract labor, increased reliance on technology, and a decrease in hiring "for new lawyers in large firms and lawyers in government practice."[3] These shifts in employment patterns and contexts mean that future faculty members and professionals are aware that they may be using their scholarly skills differently than they had originally envisioned and often in ways that require them to tap into scholarly expertise beyond how they were trained in their doctoral or professional preparation programs.

A second trend has been the shift in perceptions among doctoral students and early career scholars concerning the overall attractiveness of careers as faculty members in higher education and in some professional areas, such as medicine, the law, and nursing.[4] Doctoral students are observing the pace of work and the reported stress experienced by their faculty advisors, and at least some are asserting their preference for or commitment to a life characterized by a sense of balance between personal and professional responsibilities. Some are reassessing whether securing prestigious, tenure-track faculty posts with high expectations for publication productivity is their goal.

For some, attractive careers are those that enable them to use their scholarly talents in a wide array of roles and in contexts beyond formal higher education. The legal profession also has become less attractive as concerns about work-life balance, discrimination (for women and underrepresented minorities), and the hard-driving "billable hour" culture of law firms continue to be expressed. The decline in the attractiveness of academic and other professional careers has been partly the result of concerns about narrow definitions of how success is defined and assessed for scholars working in various professional and academic contexts. Boyer pointed out that "broadening scholarship has implications not only for individuals but for institutions, too."[5] He urged institutions to "define [their] own special mission and develop a system of faculty recognition that relates to what the campus is seeking to accomplish."[6] He then went on to suggest that the four categories of his framework could be used to start these conversations.

A third trend with implications for doctoral education in particular has been the level of national concern about the quality of undergraduate education, especially in the sciences, technology, engineering, and mathematics (STEM) fields but also in the social sciences, humanities, and professional fields. Parents, employers, and students themselves, as well as state legislators and national leaders, have called for more attention to the quality of teaching and the learning experiences of undergraduates. The scholarship of teaching, as described by Boyer, recognizes the importance and legitimacy of the teaching mission of higher education. Boyer argued for the important role that this type of scholarship can and does play in providing excellent learning experiences for undergraduates.

For example, since the 1990s, a number of reports have highlighted the nation's need for a strong pathway to prepare scientists and engineers. These reports have raised questions about challenges to the persistence and stability of that pipeline along with an overall concern about the ways in which the experiences of undergraduates in STEM fields are not serving to attract and retain talented young people.[7] Such reports often have expressed concern about didactic teaching styles that compromise student interest and engagement, and they call for more attention to teaching as a critically important scholarly role that should be informed by knowledge of current evidence-based practices. Similarly, those involved in legal education have expressed concern about the lack of attention to teaching students how to apply critical thinking within the context of legal practice and to helping future attorneys develop the social and ethical skills and judgment needed across a career.[8]

Regardless of program type, doctoral and professional graduate programs are in the business of preparing professionals to think and act like professionals in their respective fields. The aforementioned trends have had important implications for the educational experiences of graduate students in doctoral and various professional programs. The ideas advanced in *Scholarship Reconsidered* have interacted with and influenced these trends, permeating higher education and influencing thinking and reform efforts pertaining to graduate and professional education. In fact, in response to an array of concerns and ideas about the ways in which graduate and professional programs are preparing students for their future roles (and related shortcomings in this preparation), educational leaders, faculty members, and students themselves, as well as national organizations, have been calling for and engaged in major reform efforts to strengthen and improve advanced education. These calls for reform became quite strong in the 1990s and have led to a variety of innovations in graduate and professional education since then.

Within this context of critique and reform in doctoral and professional education, several themes in *Scholarship Reconsidered* have been particularly pertinent to discussions and developments. First, scholarly work takes a variety of forms. Boyer suggested a broader view of scholarship that includes teaching, synthesis, and application, as well as discovery. When scholarship is recognized to take several forms, the preparation of academics or professionals who have the ability to engage in these forms of scholarship in their fields requires the development of capability in several areas, including, among others, mastering foundational knowledge; developing skills to advance knowledge in one's field; understanding the importance of the integration and relationships among bodies of knowledge across various fields and subspecialties; knowing how to apply knowledge to problems of practice within one's field or in a cross-disciplinary context and in local, regional, national, and international communities; and demonstrating effective approaches to disseminating knowledge so that it affects practice.

Second, learning communities are contexts within which knowledge production and professional practice and learning occur. The implication for doctoral and professional programs is that they should provide communities of practice within which those preparing for work as scholars or professionals can communicate and experience opportunities to work with a variety of stakeholders. Generative and collaborative relationships between experienced scholars and those earlier in their career should characterize such learning communities.

Third, all forms of scholarship benefit from documentation and public assessment. In fact, part of scholarship is the activity of evaluating and learning from and with others. Thus, scholars should document their professional practice and should participate actively in assessment processes of their own work along with the work of others. Evaluation processes should take into account and respect all forms of scholarship, including discovery, integration, application, and teaching. Glassick, Huber, and Maeroff at the Carnegie Foundation identified six standards for assessing scholarly products of any type: clear goals, adequate preparation, appropriate methods, significant results, effective presentation, and reflective critique.[9] In preparing the next generation of scholars who will serve in faculty and professional roles, doctoral and professional education should provide opportunities for students to learn to uphold these standards in their own work along with the word of others—to document and give and receive feedback on all types of scholarly products that they produce or that their colleagues produce.

In what specific ways have the ideas offered in *Scholarship Reconsidered*, along with other factors and trends, affected doctoral and professional education? Since the 1990s, significant new developments have been incorporated into doctoral and professional education in service to expanding access, deepening learning experiences, and preparing students for the array of scholarly roles they may play in academe, industry, business, and the public sector. Several specific implications and points of impact from Boyer's work are discussed in the following.

One consequence from Boyer's work, as well as some of the other trends affecting doctoral and professional education, is the explicit acknowledgment that students in advanced degree programs face a range of career options and may follow a variety of career paths within and outside the contexts they intended. In the case of doctoral education, graduates may be involved in traditional knowledge production, teaching within academe or professional or informal settings, synthesis of knowledge in their field, or application of their expertise to practical societal problems. Furthermore, research on doctoral education highlights a growing interest among doctoral students to have an impact through their work.

The range of scholarship framed in Boyer's work highlights various avenues through which scholars can engage in meaningful and satisfying employment and has provided a vocabulary for discussing a range of options. A career focused heavily on doing the traditional research of knowledge generation, typically carried out in universities, is increasingly recognized as just one option for a scholar or professional today. A scientist, for example, may direct her expertise as a scholar to informal education with the public within a museum or a social worker may use his scholarly expertise to analyze community-based challenges to youth employment in rural communities in southern Africa. Although the tightness of the academic labor market undoubtedly has led many PhD graduates to consider various career options, Boyer's work also has contributed to a growing recognition of the variety of ways in which scholarship can be expressed.

More explicit acknowledgment of the range of career options available to doctoral graduates is leading to a growing emphasis in graduate and professional schools on explicitly preparing students for the range of career options they may consider within and outside the academy. For example, graduate schools have begun investing resources to expand staff and programming to help prepare graduate students for an array of scholarly and professional appointment types within a variety of sectors (e.g., higher education, government, and not-for-profit institutions). Examples of programming offered within graduate schools include workshops highlighting speakers who discuss a range of career options available to those with doctoral and professional degrees, fellowship programs that provide in-depth experiences for graduate students interested in the scholarship of teaching, and certificate programs that provide opportunities for students to engage in "outreach scholarship," expressions of scholarship that engage the surrounding community.

Regardless of one's profession—that of a scholar, doctor, lawyer, or other professional—and the sector of one's employment, advanced degree programs are places where professional socialization takes place. As expressed in the book describing the Carnegie Foundation's project on the doctorate, "formation ... points not only to the development of intellectual expertise but to the growth of 'the personality, character, habits of heart and mind' and 'the role that the given discipline is capable of and meant to play in academe and society at large."[10]

There is growing recognition that doctoral and professional school graduates pursue a wide array of careers within and beyond academe and, furthermore, that the pace of change in today's society means that their positions will likely change several times across a career span. Consideration of such diverse career paths, along with pressure from students concerned about the tight academic labor market in many fields, has led to more attention in doctoral and professional education to providing opportunities for students to develop the full array of skills and competencies that they will need in their future work (within and outside academe). The reform movements in doctoral, medical, and legal education have all noted a common disconnect between what students are being taught (and asked to do) and the skills they will need in their careers of choice.

Although the intellectual and scholarly practices within these fields vary, the calls for reform share some recommendations, many of which are competencies reflected in *Scholarship Reconsidered.*[11] Advanced degree programs should develop individuals who can contribute to solving problems in local, regional, national, and international contexts; be flexible in how they engage in professional practice; contribute and benefit from ongoing learning within professional communities; build, integrate, apply, and share knowledge within their work contexts; and document their professional practice by actively participating in assessment of their own professional work and that of colleagues.

Recognition has increased that advanced study should prepare students for the wide array of scholarly work in which they may engage in their fields and the diversity of employment positions that they may occupy. In response, graduate schools and academic departments have begun providing resources to help students identify and prioritize career competencies they should develop and map their progress toward mastering these skills. Law and medical schools have introduced clinical experiences earlier in the curriculum and graduate schools have begun to offer professional-preparation programs for students interested in careers in the academy (e.g., Michigan State's Center for Academic and Future Faculty Excellence—http://caffe.grd.msu.edu/) and for those still exploring the variety of ways in which they might apply and integrate the intellectual practices from graduate school in a future career (e.g., Michigan State University's PREP program—http://careersuccess.msu.edu/prep).

Efforts to reform higher education have not only occurred at the level of individual institutions. Several national initiatives have emerged as the result of public- and private-sector funds encouraging institutions to collaborate and thus improve doctoral education in ways that recognize the range of scholarly work in which doctoral graduates are likely to engage. Boyer's ideas about various forms of scholarship echo through these initiatives. Examples include the Carnegie Initiative on the Doctorate (http://gallery.carnegiefoundation.org/cid/); the Center for the Integration of Research, Teaching, and Learning (CIRTL) (www.cirtl.net); the Council of Graduate Schools' Preparing Future Faculty to Assess Student Learning Initiative (www.cgsnet.org/preparing-future-facultypreparing-future-faculty-assess-student-learning); and the programs offered by disciplinary associations to prepare the next generation of faculty members to be effective teachers and engaged scholars who can translate their work in ways that affect practice.

CIRTL is one example of a national initiative informed by Boyer's vision of scholarship and designed to reform doctoral education. A center funded by the National Science Foundation and involving more than twenty universities, CIRTL's mission is to prepare the next generation of STEM doctoral students to be excellent teachers as well as talented researchers. One of the core ideas of CIRTL, which is central to the professional development offered through CIRTL to doctoral students, is Teaching-as-Research (TAR). In particular, this concept emphasizes that teaching is a form of scholarship, as is knowledge discovery, and can be improved through efforts to ask questions and gather data about students' learning. This and other initiatives are preparing a significant number of young scholars (doctoral students) who have the commitment, values, ability, and skills to engage in the full range of scholarly activity advanced by Boyer in *Scholarship Reconsidered.*

Major cross-national initiatives in professional education have actively engaged a variety of stakeholders in recent years, including the American Medical Association's Accelerating Change in Medical Education Initiative (www.ama-assn.org/sub/accelerating-change/overview.shtml). Initiatives at participating medical schools across the country will help prepare students to better serve local communities and engage in professional collaboration with interdisciplinary groups of colleagues. This is an example of another national initiative that reflects Boyer's commitment to the acknowledgment and rewarding of a diverse range of intellectual and professional practices.

Boyer's work created an awareness and appreciation for the various forms that scholarship can take and the need for dedicated scholars prepared to engage, at high levels of excellence, in each of these scholarly paths. The landscape of doctoral and professional education has seen lively discussion and innovation in the past few decades as faculty members, students, and other stakeholders have wrestled with the outcomes of advanced education and the approaches and strategies to prepare students for their future careers. Boyer's ideas have made important contributions to discussions of how to prepare doctoral and professional students for careers in discovering new knowledge, engaging with an array of learners, improving teaching and learning experiences in their fields, connecting knowledge from within and across different disciplines, and addressing the challenging problems confronting humankind at this time in our history. As a powerful force stimulating discussion and debate about the meaning of scholarly work, *Scholarship Reconsidered* has combined with other factors at work in higher education to contribute to an environment in which doctoral and professional education has been the site of much reform and innovation over the past two decades.

As stated at the start of this chapter, *Scholarship Reconsidered* has served as a call for action within higher education, with important implications for those learning, providing, and experiencing doctoral and professional education. Alongside and interacting with several other factors and forces discussed in this chapter, the ideas in *Scholarship Reconsidered* have contributed to interest in reforming and improving doctoral and professional education to make it more relevant to the careers that academics and professionals will enter. In particular, the ideas in *Scholarship Reconsidered* and other powerful trends affecting doctoral and professional education have led to explicit recognition that students in advanced degree programs will face diverse and changing career options, challenges, and responsibilities and thus need to develop an array of abilities and competencies. In addition to developing deep knowledge in one's field, these competencies, attitudes, and abilities, echoing emphases found in *Scholarship Reconsidered,* include an understanding that scholarly talents may take many forms, the ability to share and connect one's expertise with that of others in order to apply knowledge in service to solving problems, skills in assessing one's own work and that of others, an attitude of flexibility, and a commitment to ongoing learning. Doctoral and professional programs, as well as national organizations and associations, are developing new ways to help future academics and professionals develop this array of skills and abilities that will mark them as the scholars and professionals needed in today's challenging and changing academic and professional workplaces.

HOW *SCHOLARSHIP RECONSIDERED* DISRUPTED THE PROMOTION AND TENURE SYSTEM

KerryAnn O'Meara

Many years ago for my doctoral dissertation, I studied college and university campuses that revised their promotion and tenure policies to reflect Ernest L. Boyer's broader definition of scholarship.[1] Shortly into my defense, a spirited debate emerged in the room regarding one of my engaged scholar participants. I was asked, "Would the broader definition of scholarship and revised tenure policy have been important if the scholar in question had completed the requisite number of journal articles or books *and* was involved in the scholarship of engagement on top of [his or her] traditional work? In other words, was Boyer simply trying to make an argument for faculty who could not 'cut it' as traditional scholars?"

I share this story because the question gets to the heart of Boyer's contributions to the national conversation about scholarship and reward systems. As a result, I pose several questions:

- Did Boyer's *Scholarship Reconsidered* influence what actually counts as scholarship for tenure and promotion?
- Did Boyer's *Scholarship Reconsidered* add to the legitimacy of forms of scholarship, other than discovery, within academic reward systems?
- What key point did Boyer make that has received little to no attention in substantive efforts to reform faculty member roles and rewards?

- What contexts threaten the continued impact of Boyer's broader definition of scholarship? What contexts offer hope for its adoption and expansion?

Since Boyer's *Scholarship Reconsidered* was published in 1990, there have been several pieces of work trying to extend and fill out Boyer's framework and definitions of scholarship,[2] as well as studies investigating the impact of this work within academic cultures and reward systems.[3] Overall findings suggest that the scholarship of discovery endures as the most "legitimate and preferred form of scholarship," though Boyer's work has added to what is counted as legitimate scholarship.[4]

Although Boyer's *Scholarship Reconsidered* is a widely read and cited work and has led to some important changes in academia, it could not overcome generations of academic socialization privileging the scholarship of discovery.[5] The privileged position of the scholarship of discovery is maintained through graduate student socialization and also through market forces across higher education institutions that maintain traditional forms of scholarship as the strongest, portable currency and form of transferrable social capital.[6] Such a market is maintained by routine practices such as job searches, criteria used in annual *US News & World Report (USNWR)* rankings, disciplinary awards, and social networks, and hidden controls within reward systems that reproduce narratives regarding the primacy of traditional scholarship.[7]

However, it is also true that the faculty roles and rewards reform movement led by R. Eugene Rice and Russell Edgerton (formerly of the American Association of Higher Education [AAHE]), Lee Shulman of the Carnegie Foundation, and Ernest Lynton of the New England Resource Center of Higher Education spurred hundreds of college and university campuses to reform promotion and tenure language to include a broader definition of scholarship. I studied such reforms in my dissertation,[8] with Rice through case studies of individual campus reform processes and outcomes,[9] and through a survey of four-year university provosts.[10] Provosts who implemented these reforms at their campuses were more likely than provosts at campuses that did not put these reforms in place to observe faculty member acceptance of multiple forms of scholarship.[11] Provosts who initiated reforms reported faculty members engaged in alternative forms of scholarship had better chances of being successful after the promotion and tenure reforms were put in place.[12]

These same provosts also noted such policy changes helped their campuses become more distinctive rather than mimicking the faculty standards at aspirational peers. Such findings are important to understanding the potential benefits of reward system reform as suggested by Boyer. Yet, they are limited. For example, there is not a national database of the number of engaged and teaching scholars who went up for promotion and tenure in the twenty years since such policies were put in place. As such it is not clear how many faculty members succeeded or failed in "making their case."[13] We also do not know which engaged faculty members left their respective institutions or stayed based on what was in those reformed guidelines.

Given that the rate of promotion and tenure is relatively high for those who make it to the tenure decision (seven in ten in research universities and higher in most other institutional types),[14] it could be argued that the issue is less whether publicly engaged scholars and teaching scholars are tenured in reformed reward systems and more whether their careers overall are thriving as much as those of traditional scholars. To understand this, we might identify a group of engaged graduate students who want to be faculty members. One example would be the Publicly Engaged Graduate Education program of Imagining America. This group could be paired with a control group of more traditionally minded academics who want to be faculty members and track both group's recruitment into faculty positions, retention to tenure decision, retention to promotion to full-professor status, awards, grants, and other career outcomes such as satisfaction with career.

What we know from analysis of promotion and tenure policies in four-year universities is that Boyer's *Scholarship Reconsidered* changed what many universities codified in policy as "counting" as legitimate knowledge.[15] Indeed, one of Boyer's greatest contributions to higher education was legitimacy for a new way of understanding scholarship.

Boyer's *Scholarship Reconsidered* added legitimacy to engaged, interdisciplinary, and teaching scholarship within and across higher education institutions. Scott notes legitimacy is "not a commodity to be possessed or exchanged but a condition reflecting cultural alignment, normative support, or consonance with relevant rules or laws."[16] As cultural resource-driven organizations, higher education institutions maintain and reproduce a currency of legitimacy, prestige, and reputation.[17]

Boyer added legitimacy to forms of scholarship other than discovery by breaking a long silence regarding alternative views of how to define and assess quality scholarship.[18] Specifically, Boyer disrupted the dominant narrative that there is only one kind of scholarship and one way to assess its quality. In other words, Boyer disrupted what Rice,[19] and later I,[20] referred to as the "assumptive world of the academic professional" by critiquing its very operating assumptions. By positioning scholarship as work that involves faculty expertise, peer review, and impact, rather than simply work that is published in specific journals and book presses, Boyer opened up possibilities and discussion about other forms of scholarly expression and products.

Boyer also added to the legitimacy of multiple forms of scholarship by contributing language. One of Ernest Boyer's greatest legacies was providing a foundational language for defining what scholarship is (and is not) that did not exist before *Scholarship Reconsidered.* This language of discovery, integration, teaching and transmission, and application (later changed to engagement) of knowledge remains in hundreds of promotion and tenure policies, candidate dossiers, national associations, and research today.

By providing a language for scholarship, and one that presented the different forms of knowing as equal and complementary, Boyer provided an opening, a public space, and an opportunity for higher education scholars who wanted to argue that there were more kinds of scholarship, more ways to assess quality. Boyer used his own bully pulpit as well, a strong voice coming from a major foundation president saying that there are other multiple, legitimate ways of knowing and being a scholar. The gifts of language, public space, and credibility to claim another view of knowledge making conferred legitimacy on those who had long been involved in alternative forms of scholarship without a voice and without credibility.

One of the reasons alternative forms of scholarship were marginalized at the time *Scholarship Reconsidered* was written was that these activities were considered unskilled work. Skilled work has always received greater status within organizations than unskilled work.[21] At the time of *Scholarship Reconsidered*'s release, research was the primary form of skilled work—for which there is a lengthy and specific doctoral training with clear measurable outputs. By contrast, teaching and service had fewer legitimate knowledge communities and few measurable outputs.[22] Those engaging in the scholarship of teaching and engagement did not have mature professional communities to socialize new scholars, present their work and receive peer review, provide consensus around quality and mediocre work, and confirm awards. They thus had few measurable outputs.

An entire movement has arisen from Boyer's early efforts to professionalize and increase the stature and assessment of engaged scholarship, the scholarship of teaching, and interdisciplinary research and training. Key actors in this movement include the Carnegie Foundation, the New England Resource Center for Higher Education, Imagining America, Community-Campus Partnerships for Health, CIRTL, and the

International Association for Research on Service-Learning and Community Engagement (IARSCLE). Scholars involved in newer forms of scholarship rolled up their sleeves and created professional networks for faculty members and administrators, graduate school training, journals, and recognition systems. They began to form knowledge-sharing and knowledge-creating professional communities that provide recognition and legitimacy for this work.

Boyer also provided higher education faculty members a language for talking about inequalities that exist within reward systems. This was also a disruption. Jencks and Riesman had warned of the dangers of isomorphism in higher education in which every four-year university tries to mimic the standards of Harvard and in doing so loses its distinctiveness.[23] Boyer's work ignited conversations on college and university campuses about the kinds of scholarship that were being valorized within institutional reward systems and those that were being marginalized. Boyer pointed out that many of the forms of knowledge making that were being marginalized were those that were most communal and collective in nature. Competitive individualism and elite notions of appropriate university research had taken over reward systems to disenfranchise knowledge making that was collaborative, interdisciplinary, engaged with public problems, and in partnership with students. Although Boyer advocated that faculty members be able to engage in all kinds of scholarship, including discovery, he made the argument that the purposes of higher education were not served by a singular, individualistic form of scholarship or inequalities in how these different kinds of knowledge making were legitimized, valued, and rewarded.[24]

The contribution that Boyer made to the legitimacy of newer forms of scholarship cannot be overestimated, and I think they will stand the test of time. To me this contribution stands beside the work of Barr and Tagg[25] in providing language for a shift from a teaching to a learning paradigm and the work of the National Survey of Student Engagement (NSSE) in getting higher education to understand the value of "high-impact practices" for students. They are contributions that we cannot forget or retreat from but reside in our collective consciousness as a form of accountability and claimed intellectual space.

Despite the fact that Boyer's *Scholarship Reconsidered* was closely read, influential on policy, and is one of the mostly widely cited pieces of scholarship on higher education, several important points made by Ernest Boyer were not given the attention they deserved. The most important of the overlooked points, in my view, is the idea that reward systems need to be reformed so that faculty members get more credit for the work that they do every day that is not scholarship. Boyer makes the point that mentoring, effective teaching, and shared governance, for example, are all critical to the ongoing development and excellence of higher education.[26] Each time a faculty member sits with a student in a coffee shop for two hours helping him or her discern a career direction, supervises a program's accreditation process, deliberates over general education requirements, or mentors other faculty members, he or she contributes to his or her institution's goals.

It is not only the research our higher education faculty members engage in that has made the American system of higher education one of the best systems in the world but also our systems of shared governance and commitment to a holistic development of students. A concrete application of Boyer's admonition to recognize nonscholarly tasks would have been to reform promotion and tenure so that the portion of scholarship required (that is, any scholarship) is less and teaching and shared governance count more. This has not been done for many reasons.

There are many forces that have threatened and will continue to do so the long-term impact of a broader definition of scholarship in higher education institutions; I will mention only a few here. First, national and world ranking systems that emphasize faculty member publications, citation counts, fellowships, and more traditional indicators of faculty research productivity create a disincentive for valuing nontraditional scholarship in faculty member reward system.[27] Second, efforts by institutions to "strive," to move up in rankings and prestigious membership associations, threaten more regional connections between universities and communities and between students and faculty members who produce excellent engaged scholarship and teaching scholarship.[28]

The greatest threat to the idea of faculty members being rewarded for a "mosaic of talent" in knowledge making has been the rise in non-tenure-track faculty member appointments and the unbundling of faculty member roles. There are many concerns about working conditions and academic freedom for non-tenure-track faculty members that have emerged with the increase in these positions. However, I speak specifically here about the amount of time that non-tenure-track faculty members have built into their workload to devote to any scholarship, much less engaged, interdisciplinary, or teaching scholarship. Boyer critiqued higher education faculty members for focusing more on their scholarship than on undergraduate education, public engagement, and the development of campus communities, but Boyer did not want an employment system where a portion of the academic workforce was not given time for scholarly learning and scholarly contributions. As such, those interested in advocating for multiple forms of scholarship will need to work on multiple fronts simultaneously—continuing to try and expand what counts for tenure and promotion and finding new ways to carve out time and support for scholarship of all kinds for non-tenure-track faculty members.

To end on a more positive note, there is much hope to be found for assimilation of the broader definition of scholarship into the fabric of higher education because of the interests and passions of the newest generation of scholars.[29] Much research shows a growth in interdisciplinary majors and dissertations. National Science Foundation (NSF) programs such as IGERT, CIRTL, and AGEP PROMISE are preparing graduate students with interests in the scholarship of teaching and interdisciplinary and engaged scholarship. Imagining that America's PAGE program and NERCHE's Next Generation Engagement program are helping to prepare graduate students to navigate the academy while remaining true to their commitments to engagement reveals an emerging generation of scholars who may be able to change the strong norms and structures of disciplinary fields and higher education organizations through critical mass, persistence, and excellent scholarship in new forms.[30]

In sum, Boyer's *Scholarship Reconsidered* played an important role in reframing discussions about faculty member work. Hundreds of institutions have used the Boyer framework to revise their promotion and tenure guidelines, expanding the definition and criteria of what counts as scholarship within their reward systems. Boyer played a critical role in adding to the legitimacy of engaged scholarship and the scholarship of teaching by providing language and encouraging the development of networks and professional communities to evaluate and advance newer forms of scholarship. Today this legacy lives on in vibrant knowledge communities committed to newer forms of scholarship and to continuing to reform faculty member roles and rewards.

ACKNOWLEDGMENTS

This book reflects the work of many people, and I'd like to thank, first, Charles Glassick, Bob Hochstein, Mary Huber, and Gene Maeroff, colleagues here at the foundation who spent endless hours reviewing final drafts, providing invaluable critique, and helping with editorial revisions. Vito Perrone also joined frequently in this process and provided sharply focused comments and suggestions. I am deeply indebted to these associates for their wonderfully helpful contributions.

I also wish to thank, in a very special way, my colleague Eugene Rice, currently dean of the faculty at Antioch College. Gene joined the foundation as senior fellow just as our report on the professoriate was beginning to take shape. He made contributions to this report for which I am grateful—proposing, for example, that the four categories of scholarship as I had originally defined them be placed in larger context, using Ralph Waldo Emerson's essay, *The American Scholar,* as a point of reference. In the end, our work evolved into two separate books. My own report, *Scholarship Reconsidered: Priorities of the Professoriate,* restricts the discussion largely to issues *within* the academy itself. A forthcoming report, *The New American Scholar,* will make it possible for Dr. Rice to explore, in greater depth, the relationship of scholarship to the changing social context and the emerging debate about "ways of knowing." I look forward to Dr. Rice's study that surely will enrich the debate about the meaning of scholarship in contemporary life.

The contributions other colleagues made to this report also should be noted. Stanley Katz, president of the American Council of Learned Societies, deserves special mention. He, with his colleague Douglas Greenberg, agreed to organize a special seminar to critique the manuscript, and in July 1990 we were joined here in Princeton, New Jersey, by the following distinguished scholars: Marianne H. Begemann, Charles Bray, Daniel Fallon, James O. Freedman, Richard Slotkin, Hugo Sonnenschein, Joan Hinde Stewart, Catharine R. Stimpson, John Strassburger, Uri Treisman, and Margaret Wilkerson. For two days these outstanding scholars reviewed the manuscript, and their insightful comments led to significant revision of the text.

Russell Edgerton, president of the American Association for Higher Education, has contributed more to the report than he will ever know. Soon after *College* was released, Russ talked to many about the need to focus on faculty. He encouraged us to prepare a special report on the work of the professoriate and this year selected scholarship as the theme of the 1990 AAHE convention, arranged a special luncheon with key colleagues to discuss a draft of our report, and later on, carefully critiqued the manuscript. I am most grateful to Russ for his wisdom and wonderfully helpful insights.

Mary Jean Whitelaw and Lois Harwood also were valuable contributors. These colleagues reviewed carefully Carnegie faculty [member] surveys and helped select tables that related most directly to the report. Hinda Greenberg and Jan Hempel, assisted by Joanna Foster, were responsible for the bibliographical work. I'm most grateful for the wonderful help these associates have given.

Midway through our study, Irving Spitzberg and Virginia Thomdike conducted a survey of academic leaders to learn about current practices in the faculty system of recognitions and rewards. Their findings were most informative and assisted us in considering issues around faculty evaluation.

I thank Richard I. Miller, Hongyu Chen, Jerome B. Hart, and Clyde B. Killian for making available to us data from their unpublished survey on faculty attitudes toward their professional activities.

As the manuscript was taking final shape, I sent it to Warren Bryan Martin, Paul Boyer, and Ernest Boyer Jr. for critique. In response I received clear, well-focused comments and rich editorial suggestions that strengthened substantially the report.

Several other people must be given recognition. Laura Bell, Dawn Ott, and Kelli Lanino were responsible for processing innumerable drafts of the manuscript, meeting impossible deadlines. They remained wholly professional and wonderfully good spirited throughout. Dee Sanders supervised the word processing team, assisted with the design, and, along with Carol Lasala, conducted the meticulous work of producing camera-ready pages. This report is a tribute to their dedicated efforts.

Jan Hempel was responsible for copy editing and design, moving the book from manuscript to publication. It was Jan who managed the endless details necessary for the completion of the project, working closely with the press, and I am deeply grateful for her contribution to this project.

Finally, I thank Kay, my wife, for believing in the importance of this project, for encouraging me to write, and for, once again, graciously surrendering precious family time so deadlines could be met.

Ernest L. Boyer
President
The Carnegie Foundation
for the Advancement of Teaching

PART TWO

SCHOLARSHIP RECONSIDERED BY ERNEST L. BOYER

SCHOLARSHIP OVER TIME

Several years ago, while completing our study of undergraduate education, it became increasingly clear that one of the most crucial issues—the one that goes to the core of academic life—relates to the meaning of scholarship itself. In *College: The Undergraduate Experience in America,* we said, "Scholarship is not an esoteric appendage; it is at the heart of what the profession is all about..." and "to weaken faculty commitment for scholarship... is to undermine the undergraduate experience, regardless of the academic setting."[1] The challenge, as we saw it, was to define the work of faculty in ways that enrich, rather than restrict, the quality of campus life.

Today, on campuses across the nation, there is a recognition that the faculty reward system does not match the full range of academic functions and that professors are often caught between competing obligations. In response, there is a lively and growing discussion about how faculty should, in fact, spend their time. Recently, Stanford University president Donald Kennedy called for more contact between faculty and students, especially in the junior and senior years, a time when career decisions are more likely to be made. "It is time," Kennedy said, "for us to reaffirm that education—that is, teaching in all its forms—is the primary task" of higher education.[2]

Several years ago, the University of California completed a study of undergraduate education, recommending that more weight be placed on teaching in faculty tenure decisions.[3] In the East, the University of Pennsylvania, in its faculty handbook, now states that "the teaching of students at all levels is to be distributed among faculty members without regard to rank or seniority as such."[4] In the Midwest, Robert Gavin, president of Macalester College, recently reaffirmed his institution's view of the liberal arts mission as including not only academic quality but also internationalism, diversity, and service.[5]

It is *this* issue—what it means to be a scholar—that is the central theme of our report. The time has come, we believe, to step back and reflect on the variety of functions academics are expected to perform. It's time to ask how priorities of the professoriate relate to the faculty reward system, as well as to the missions of America's higher learning institutions. Such an inquiry into the work of faculty is essential if students are to be well served, if the creativity of all faculty is to be fully tapped, and if the goals of every college and university are to be appropriately defined.

While we speak with pride about the great diversity of American higher education, the reality is that on many campuses standards of scholarship have become increasingly restrictive, and campus priorities frequently are more imitative than distinctive. In this climate, it seems appropriate to ask: How can each of the nation's colleges and universities define, with clarity, its own special purposes? Should expectations regarding faculty performance vary from one type of institution to another? Can we, in fact, have a higher education system in this country that includes multiple models of success?

Other issues within the academy must be candidly confronted. For example, the administrative structure has grown more and more complex, the disciplines have become increasingly divided, and academic departments frequently are disconnected from one another. The curriculum is fragmented, and the educational experience of students frequently lacks coherence. Many are now asking: How can the work of the nation's colleges and universities become more intellectually coherent? Is it possible for scholarship to be defined in ways that give more recognition to interpretative and integrative work?

According to the dominant view, to be a scholar is to be a researcher—and publication is the primary yardstick by which scholarly productivity is measured. At the same time, evidence abounds that many professors feel ambivalent about their roles. This conflict of academic functions demoralizes the professoriate, erodes the vitality of the institution, and cannot help but have a negative impact on students. Given these tensions, what is the balance to be struck between teaching and research? Should some members of the professoriate be thought of primarily as researchers and others as teachers? And how can these various dimensions of faculty work be more appropriately evaluated and rewarded?

Beyond the campus, America's social and economic crises are growing—troubled schools, budget deficits, pollution, urban decay, and neglected children, to highlight problems that are most apparent. Other concerns such as acid rain, AIDS, dwindling energy supplies, and population shifts are truly global, transcending national boundaries. Given these realities, the conviction is growing that the vision of service that once so energized the nation's campuses must be given a new legitimacy. The challenge then is this: Can America's colleges and universities, with all the richness of their resources, be of greater service to the nation and the world? Can we define scholarship in ways that respond more adequately to the urgent new realities both within the academy and beyond?

Clearly, the educational and social issues now confronting the academy have changed profoundly since the first college was planted on this continent more than 350 years ago. Challenges on the campus and in society have grown, and there is a deepening conviction that the role of higher education, as well as the priorities of the professoriate, must be redefined to reflect new realities.

Looking back, one can see that scholarship in American higher education has moved through three distinct, yet overlapping, phases. The colonial college, with its strong British roots, took a view of collegiate life that focused on the student on building character and preparing new generations for civic and religious leadership. One of the first goals the English settlers of Massachusetts pursued, said the author of a description of the founding of Harvard College in 1636, was to "advance *Learning* and perpetuate it to Posterity."[6] Harvard College, patterned after Emmanuel College of Cambridge, England, was founded to provide a continuous supply of learned clergy for "the city on the hill" that the Massachusetts Puritans hoped would bring redemptive light to all mankind.

The colonial college was expected to educate and morally uplift the coming generation. Teaching was viewed as a vocation—a sacred calling—an act of dedication honored as fully as the ministry. Indeed, what society expected of faculty was largely dictated by the religious purposes of the colleges that employed them. Students were entrusted to tutors responsible for their intellectual, moral, and spiritual development. According to historian Theodore Benditt, "professors were hired not for their scholarly ability or achievement but for their religious commitment. Scholarly achievement was not a high priority, either for professors or students."[7]

This tradition, one that affirmed the centrality of teaching, persisted well into the nineteenth century. Young scholars continued to be the central focus of collegiate life, and faculty were employed with the understanding that they would be educational mentors, both in the classroom and beyond. In 1869, the image of the scholar as *teacher* was evoked by Charles W. Eliot, who, upon assuming the presidency of Harvard College, declared that "the prime business of American professors ... must be regular and assiduous class teaching."[8]

But change was in the wind. A new country was being formed and higher education's focus began to shift from the shaping of young lives to the building of a nation. As historian Frederick Rudolf says of the new generation of educators: "All were touched by the American faith in tomorrow, in the unquestionable capacity of Americans to achieve a better world."[9] It was in this climate that Rensselaer Polytechnic Institute [RPI] in Troy, New York, one of the nation's first technical schools, was founded in 1824. RPI became, according to Rudolf, "a constant reminder that the United States needed railroad-builders, bridge-builders, builders of all kinds, and that the institute in Troy was prepared to create them even if the old institutions were not."[10]

In 1846, Yale University authorized the creation of a professorship of "agricultural chemistry and animal and vegetable physiology."[11] In the same decade, Harvard president Edward Everett stressed his institution's role in the service of business and economic prosperity. The college took Everett's message to heart. When historian Henry Adams asked his students why they had come to study at Cambridge, the answer he got was unambiguous: "The degree of Harvard College is worth money to me in Chicago."[12]

The practical side of higher learning was remarkably enhanced by the Morrill Act of 1862, later called the Land Grant College Act. This historic piece of legislation gave federal land to each state, with proceeds from sale of the land to support both education in the liberal arts and training in the skills that ultimately would undergird the emerging agricultural and mechanical revolutions. The Hatch Act of 1887 added energy to the effort by providing federal funds to create university-sponsored agricultural experiment stations that brought learning to the farmer, and the idea of education as a democratic function to serve the common good was planted on the prairies.

Something of the excitement of this era was captured in Willa Cather's description of her fellow students and her teachers at the University of Nebraska in the 1890s: "[They] came straight from the cornfields with only summer's wages in their pockets, hung on through four years, shabby and underfed, and completed the course by really heroic self-sacrifice. Our instructors were oddly assorted: wandering pioneer school teachers, stranded ministers of the Gospel, a few enthusiastic young men just out of graduate school. There was an atmosphere of endeavor, of expectancy and bright hopefulness about the young college that had lifted its head from the prairie only a few years ago."[13]

Thus, American higher education, once devoted primarily to the intellectual and moral development of students, added *service* as a mission, and both private and public universities took up the challenge. In 1903, David Starr Jordan, president of Stanford University, declared that the entire university movement in the twentieth century "is toward reality and practicality."[14] By 1908, Harvard president Charles Eliot could claim: "At bottom most of the American institutions of higher education are filled with the modem democratic spirit of serviceableness. Teachers and students alike are profoundly moved by the desire to serve the democratic community.... All the colleges boast of the serviceable men they have trained, and regard the serviceable patriot as their ideal product. This is a thoroughly democratic conception of their function."[15]

Skeptics looked with amusement, even contempt, at what they considered the excesses of utility and accommodation. They long resisted the idea of making the university itself a more democratic institution and viewed with disdain Ezra Cornell's soaring pledge in the 1860s to "...found an institution 'where any person can find instruction in any study.'"[16] Some critics even viewed the agricultural experiment stations as a betrayal of higher education's mission. They ridiculed the "cow colleges," seeing in them a dilution of academic standards. Others recoiled from the idea that non-elite young people were going on to college.[17]

Still, a host of academics flocked to land-grant colleges, confident they had both the expertise and the obligation to contribute to building a nation. They embodied the spirit of Emerson, who years before had spoken of the scholarship of "action" as "the raw material out of which the intellect moulds her splendid products."[18] In this tradition, Governor Robert LaFollette forged, in Wisconsin, a powerful link between the campus and the state, one that became known nationally as the "Wisconsin Idea."[19] After visiting Madison in 1909, social critic Lincoln Steffens observed: " In Wisconsin the university is as close to the intelligent farmer as his pig-pen or his tool-house; the university laboratories are part of the alert manufacturer's plant...."[20]

The idea that professors could spread knowledge that would improve agriculture and manufacturing gave momentum to what later became known as *applied* research. In the 1870s and 1880s, many agreed that education was, above all, to be considered useful. In commenting on the link between the campus and applied agricultural research, historian Margaret Rossiter presented this vivid illustration: "The chief activities of a professor of agriculture ... were to run field tests with various fertilizers and to maintain a model farm, preferably, but rarely, without financial loss."[21] Over the next thirty years, these agricultural sciences developed at a rapid pace, vastly increasing the knowledge that scholars could apply.

Service during this expansive period had a moral meaning, too. The goal was not only to *serve* society, but *reshape* it. Andrew White, the first president of Cornell University, saw graduates "pouring into the legislatures, staffing the newspapers, and penetrating the municipal and county boards of America. Corruption would come to an end; pure American ideals would prosper until one day they governed the entire world."[22] Sociologist Edward Shils, in describing the spirit of the times, observed that "the concept of improvement was vague and comprehensive, signifying not only improvement of a practical sort but spiritual improvement as well."[23]

This ideal—the conviction that higher education had a moral mission to fulfill—was especially important to those who organized the American Economic Association in 1885, under the leadership of Richard Ely. Soon after joining the newly formed faculty at Johns Hopkins University, Ely wrote to the president, Daniel Coit Gilman, that the fledgling association would help in the diffusion of "a sound Christian political economy."[24] Most faculty were less zealous. Still, in this remarkable era marked by continued emphasis on liberal education and values, the faculty role was energized by determined efforts to apply knowledge to practical problems.

Basic research, a third dimension of scholarly activity, which can be traced to the first years of the Republic, also began to take hold. The earliest research effort was largely led by investigators *outside* the academy—people such as Thomas Jefferson, the mathematician Nathaniel Bowditch, the pioneer botanists John and William Bartram, and the intrepid astronomer Maria Mitchell, who set up an observatory on lonely Nantucket Island and, on one October night in 1847, discovered a new comet. When President Jefferson sought a scientific leader for the first of the great western explorations, he did not go to the colleges, where science was not yet well developed. Instead, he looked within government and selected his personal secretary, Meriwether Lewis, who was known to have a keen eye for the natural word. Before the expedition, Lewis was sent to Philadelphia, where he received careful training in astronomy, botany, and mineralogy from members of the American Philosophical Society.[25]

Still, colleges themselves were not wholly devoid of scientific effort. As early as 1738, John Winthrop of Harvard, the first academic scientist, had a laboratory in which to conduct experiments. He later persuaded the lawmakers in Massachusetts to sponsor America's first astronomical expedition. These early scientists traveled to Newfoundland in 1761 to observe the transit of Venus.[26] Moreover, George Ticknor and Edward Everett, who attended a German university in 1815, are believed to have been the first Americans to go abroad to pursue advanced scholarly studies. Upon their return, they called, even then, for the introduction at Harvard of the German approach to scholarship.[27]

Yet, change came slowly. The new sciences were very much on the edges of academic life and expectations were modest. As Dael Wolfle wrote: "Professors were hired to teach the science that was already known—to add to that knowledge was not expected..."[28] Consider also that when Benjamin Silliman became the first chemistry professor at Yale in 1802, there were only twenty-one other full-time scientific faculty positions in the United States.[29]

By the mid-nineteenth century, however, leading Atlantic seaboard colleges were giving more legitimacy to the authority of scientific effort and a few were beginning to transform themselves into research and graduate institutions. For example, Harvard's Lawrence Scientific School and Yale's Sheffield Scientific School were forerunners of the academy's deep commitment to the scholarship of science. Graduate courses in philosophy and the arts were established, and America's first [d]octor of [p]hilosophy was conferred at Yale in 1861.[30] And the Massachusetts Institute of Technology, which opened its doors at the end of the Civil War, soon was recognized as a center of scientific investigation.

In the late nineteenth century, more Americans who, like Ticknor and Everett, had studied in Europe were profoundly influenced by the research orientation of the German university and wanted to develop a similar model here.[31] G. Stanley Hall, first president of Clark University, wrote in 1891, "The German University is today the freest spot on earth.... Nowhere has the passion to push on to the frontier of human knowledge been so general."[32] Some, it is true, resisted the German influences. The prominent American humanist Irving Babbitt argued that the PhD degree led to a loss of balance. He complained about the "maiming and mutilation of the mind that comes from over-absorption in one subject," declaring that German doctoral dissertations gave him " a sort of intellectual nausea."[33]

Still, research and graduate education increasingly formed the model for the modem university. Academics on both continents were moving inevitably from faith in authority to reliance on scientific rationality. And to men like Daniel Coit Gilman, this view of scholarship called for a new kind of university, one based on the conviction that knowledge was most attainable through research and experimentation. Acting on this conviction, Gilman founded Johns Hopkins University in 1876, a step described by Shils as "perhaps the single, most decisive event in the history of learning in the Western hemisphere."[34]

In the 1870s, the universities of Pennsylvania, Harvard, Columbia, and Princeton, in that order, also began to offer programs leading to the PhD degree, and the University of Chicago, founded in 1891, made the degree "the pinnacle of the academic program."[35] By 1895 William Rainey Harper, president of this newly formed university, could require "each appointee to sign an agreement that his promotions in rank and salary would depend chiefly upon his research productivity."[36]

By the late nineteenth century, the advancement of knowledge through *research* had taken firm root in American higher education, and colonial college values, which emphasized teaching undergraduates, began to lose ground to the new university that was emerging. Indeed, the founders of Johns Hopkins University considered restricting study on that campus to the graduate level only. In the end, some undergraduate education proved necessary, but the compromise was reluctantly made, and for many professors, class and lecture work became almost incidental. Service, too, was viewed as unimportant. Some even considered it a violation of the integrity of the university, since the prevailing Germanic model demanded that the professor view the everyday world from a distance.

It should be stressed, however, that throughout most of American higher education the emphasis on research and graduate education remained the exception rather than the rule. The principal mission at most of the nation's colleges and universities continued to be the education of undergraduates. And the land-grant colleges, especially, took pride in service.

But in the 1940s, as the Great Depression gave way to a devastating war, the stage was set for a dramatic transformation of academic life. At that historic moment, Vannevar Bush of MIT and James Bryant Conant of Harvard volunteered the help of the universities in bringing victory to the nation. In 1940, Bush took the lead in establishing the National Defense Research Committee which, a year later, became the Office of Scientific Research and Development. Academics flocked to Washington to staff the new agencies and federal research grants began to flow.[37] Universities and the nation had joined in common cause.

After the war, Vannevar Bush urged continuing federal support for research. In a 1945 report to the [p]resident entitled *Science: The Endless Frontier,* he declared: "Science, by itself, provides no panacea for individual, social, and economic ills. It can be effective in the national welfare only as a member of a team, whether the conditions be peace or war. But without scientific progress no amount of achievement in other directions can [e]nsure our health, prosperity, and security as a nation in the modem world."[38] The case could not have been more clearly stated. Higher learning and government had, through scientific collaboration, changed the course of history—and the impact on the academy would be both consequential and enduring.

Soon, a veritable army of freshly minted PhDs fanned out to campuses across the country. Inspired by their mentors, this new generation of faculty found themselves committed not only to their institutions but also to their professions. Young scholars sought to replicate the research climate they themselves had recently experienced. Academic priorities that had for years been the inspiration of the few now became the imperative of the many. In the new climate, discipline-based departments became the foundation of faculty allegiance, and being a "scholar" was now virtually synonymous with being an academic professional. Christopher Jencks and David Riesman, capturing the spirit of that period, declared that an *academic revolution* had taken place.[39]

In 1958, Theodore Caplow and Reece McGee defined this new reality when they observed that while young faculty were hired as *teachers,* they were evaluated primarily as *researchers.*[40] This shift in expectations is vividly revealed in two national surveys conducted by the Carnegie Foundation for the Advancement of Teaching. Twenty-one percent of the faculty surveyed in 1969 strongly agreed that it is difficult to achieve tenure without publishing. By 1989, the number had doubled, to 42 percent (table 1).[41] The change at comprehensive colleges—from 6 percent to 43 percent—is especially noteworthy since these institutions have virtually no doctoral programs and only limited resources for research. Even at liberal arts colleges, where teaching has always been highly prized, nearly

TABLE 1. IN MY DEPARTMENT IT IS DIFFICULT FOR A PERSON TO ACHIEVE TENURE IF HE OR SHE DOES NOT PUBLISH

	1969	1989
All respondents	**21%**	**42%**
Research	44	83
Doctorate-granting	27	71
Comprehensive	6	43
Liberal arts	6	24
Two-year	3	4

Please see appendix C for a definition of institution classifications.

Source: The Carnegie Foundation for the Advancement of Teaching, 1969 and 1989 National Surveys of Faculty.

one in four faculty strongly agreed in 1989 that it is difficult to get tenure without publishing.

Meanwhile, the nation's colleges and universities were experiencing another remarkable social transformation—the revolution of rising expectations. In 1947, Harry S. Truman appointed a President's Commission on Higher Education and almost overnight the mission of higher education in the nation was dramatically redefined. In its landmark report, this panel of prominent citizens concluded that America's colleges and universities should no longer be "merely the instrument for producing an intellectual elite." Rather, the report stated, higher education must become "the means by which every citizen, youth, and adult, is enabled and encouraged to carry his education, formal and informal, as far as his native capacities permit."[42]

In response to this expansive vision, the nation moved from an *elite* to a *mass* system of higher education, to use sociologist Martin Trow's helpful formulation. New colleges were built, new faculty hired, and the GI Bill of Rights, first authorized in 1944, changed the entire tradition of who should go to college. Almost eight million former servicemen and -women benefited from the legislation. In the years to come, younger brothers and sisters, and eventually sons and daughters, followed in the footsteps of the veterans. Higher education, once viewed as a privilege, was now accepted as a fight.

But even as the mission of American higher education was expanding, the standards used to measure academic prestige continued to be narrowed. Increasingly, professors were expected to conduct research and publish results. Promotion and tenure depended on such activity, and young professors seeking security and status found it more rewarding—in a quite literal sense—to deliver a paper at a national convention in New York or Chicago than teach undergraduates back home. Lip service still was being paid to maintaining a balance between collegiate responsibilities and university work, but on most campuses the latter had clearly won the day.

Research per se was not the problem. The problem was that the research mission, which was appropriate for some institutions, created a shadow over the entire higher learning enterprise—and the model of a "Berkeley" or an "Amherst" became the yardstick by which all institutions would be measured. Ernest Lynton, Commonwealth Professor at the University of Massachusetts, in commenting on the new priorities, concluded that developments after the Second World War "established too narrow a definition of scholarship and too limited a range of instruction."[43] Ironically, at the very time America's higher education institutions were becoming more open and inclusive, the culture of the professoriate was becoming more hierarchical and restrictive.

Thus, in just a few decades, priorities in American higher education were significantly realigned. The emphasis on undergraduate education, which throughout the years had drawn its inspiration from the colonial college tradition, was being overshadowed by the European university tradition, with its emphasis on graduate education and research. Specifically, at many of the nation's four-year institutions, the focus had moved from the student to the professoriate, from general to specialized education, and from loyalty to the campus to loyalty to the profession.

We conclude that for America's colleges and universities to remain vital a new vision of scholarship is required. What we are faced with, today, is the need to clarify campus missions and relate the work of the academy more directly to the realities of contemporary life. We need especially to ask how institutional diversity can be strengthened and how the rich array of faculty talent in our colleges and universities might be more effectively used and continuously renewed. We proceed with the conviction that if the nation's higher learning institutions are to meet today's urgent academic and social mandates, their missions must be carefully redefined and the meaning of scholarship creatively reconsidered.

ENLARGING THE PERSPECTIVE

Since colonial times, the American professoriate has responded to mandates both from within the academy and beyond. First came teaching, then service, and finally, the challenge of research. In more recent years, faculty have been asked to blend these three traditions, but despite this idealized expectation, a wide gap now exists between the myth and the reality of academic life. Almost all colleges pay lip service to the trilogy of teaching, research, and service, but when it comes to making judgments about professional performance, the three rarely are assigned equal merit.

Today, when we speak of being "scholarly," it usually means having academic rank in a college or university and being engaged in research and publication. But we should remind ourselves just how recently the word "research" actually entered the vocabulary of higher education. The term was first used in England in the 1870s by reformers who wished to make Cambridge and Oxford "not only a place of teaching, but a place of learning," and it was later introduced to American higher education in 1906 by Daniel Coit Gilman.[1] But scholarship in earlier times referred to a variety of creative work carried on in a variety of places, and its integrity was measured by the ability to think, communicate, and learn.

What we now have is a more restricted view of scholarship, one that limits it to a hierarchy of functions. Basic research has come to be viewed as the first and most essential form of scholarly activity, with other functions flowing from it. Scholars are academics who conduct research, publish, and then perhaps convey their knowledge to students or apply what they have learned. The latter functions grow *out of* scholarship; they are not to be considered a part of it. But knowledge is not necessarily developed in such a linear manner. The arrow of causality can, and frequently does, point in *both* directions. Theory surely leads to practice. But practice also leads to theory. And teaching, at its best, shapes both research and practice. Viewed from this perspective, a more comprehensive, more dynamic understanding of scholarship can be considered, one in which the rigid categories of teaching, research, and service are broadened and more flexibly defined.

There is a readiness, we believe, to rethink what it means to be a scholar. Richard I. Miller, professor of higher education at Ohio University, recently surveyed academic vice presidents and deans at more than eight hundred colleges and universities to get their opinion about faculty functions. These administrators were asked if they thought it would be a good idea to view scholarship as more than research. The responses were overwhelmingly supportive of this proposition.[2] The need to reconsider scholarship surely goes beyond opinion polls, but campus debates, news stories, and the themes of national conventions suggest that administrative leaders are rethinking the definitions of academic life. Moreover, faculty, themselves, appear to be increasingly dissatisfied with conflicting priorities on the campus.

How then should we proceed? Is it possible to define the work of faculty in ways that reflect more realistically the full range of academic and civic mandates? We believe the time has come to move beyond the tired old "teaching versus research" debate and give the familiar and honorable term "scholarship" a broader, more capacious meaning, one that brings legitimacy to the full scope of academic work. Surely, scholarship means engaging in original research. But the work of the scholar also means stepping back from one's investigation, looking for connections, building bridges between theory and practice, and communicating one's knowledge effectively to students. Specifically, we conclude that the work of the professoriate might be thought of as having four separate, yet overlapping, functions. These are the scholarship of *discovery*, the scholarship of *integration*, the scholarship of *application*, and the scholarship of *teaching*.

The Scholarship of Discovery

The first and most familiar element in our model, the *scholarship of discovery,* comes closest to what is meant when academics speak of "research." No tenets in the academy are held in higher regard than the commitment to knowledge for its own sake, to freedom of inquiry, and to following, in a disciplined fashion, an investigation wherever it may lead. Research is central to the work of higher learning, but our study here, which inquires into the meaning of scholarship, is rooted in the conviction that disciplined, investigative efforts within the academy should be strengthened, not diminished.

The *scholarship of discovery,* at its best, contributes not only to the stock of human knowledge but also to the intellectual climate of a college or university. Not just the outcomes, but the process, and especially the passion, give meaning to the effort. The advancement of knowledge can generate an almost palpable excitement in the life of an educational institution. As William Bowen, former president of Princeton University, said, scholarly research "reflects our pressing, irrepressible need as human beings to confront the unknown and to seek understanding for its own sake. It is tied inextricably to the freedom to think freshly, to see propositions of every kind in ever-changing light. And it celebrates the special exhilaration that comes from a new idea."[3]

The list of distinguished researchers who have added luster to the nation's intellectual life would surely include heroic figures of earlier days—Yale chemist Benjamin Silliman, Harvard naturalist Louis Agassiz, astronomer William Cranch Bond, and Columbia anthropologist Franz Boas. It would also include giants of our time—James Watson, who helped unlock the genetic code; political philosopher Hannah Arendt; anthropologist Ruth Benedict; historian John Hope Franklin; geneticist Barbara McClintock; and Noam Chomsky, who transformed the field of linguistics; among others.

When the research records of higher learning are compared, the United States is the pacesetter. If we take as our measure of accomplishment the number of Nobel Prizes awarded since 1945, United States scientists received 56 percent of the awards in physics, 42 percent in chemistry, and 60 percent in medicine.[4] Prior to the outbreak of the Second World War, American scientists, including those who fled Hitler's Europe, had received only 18 of the 129 prizes in these three areas. With regard to physics, for example, a recent report by the National Research Council states: "Before World War II, physics was essentially a European activity, but by the war's end, the center of physics had moved to the United States."[5] The council goes on to review the advances in fields ranging from elementary particle physics to cosmology.

The research contribution of universities is particularly evident in medicine. Investigations in the late nineteenth century on bacteria and viruses paid off in the 1930s with the development of immunizations for diphtheria, tetanus, lobar pneumonia, and other bacterial infections. On the basis of painstaking research, a taxonomy of infectious diseases has emerged, making possible streptomycin and other antibiotics. In commenting on these breakthroughs, physician and medical writer Lewis Thomas observes: "It was basic science of a very high order, storing up a great mass of interesting knowledge for its own sake, creating, so to speak, a bank of information, ready for drawing on when the time for intelligent use arrived."[6]

Thus, the probing mind of the researcher is an incalculably vital asset to the academy and the world. Scholarly investigation, in all the disciplines, is at the very heart of academic life, and the pursuit of knowledge must be assiduously cultivated and defended. The intellectual excitement fueled by this quest enlivens faculty and invigorates higher learning institutions, and in our complicated, vulnerable world, the discovery of new knowledge is absolutely crucial.

The Scholarship of Integration

In proposing the *scholarship of integration,* we underscore the need for scholars who give meaning to isolated facts, putting them in perspective. By integration, we mean making connections across the disciplines, placing the specialties in larger context, illuminating data in a revealing way, often educating nonspecialists, too. In calling for a scholarship of integration, we do not suggest returning to the "gentleman scholar" of an earlier time, nor do we have in mind the dilettante. Rather, what we mean is serious, disciplined work that seeks to interpret, draw together, and bring new insight to bear on original research.

This more integrated view of knowledge was expressed eloquently by Mark Van Doren nearly thirty years ago when he wrote: "The connectedness of things is what the educator contemplates to the limit of his capacity.

No human capacity is great enough to permit a vision of the world as simple, but if the educator does not aim at the vision no one else will, and the consequences are dire when no one does."[7] It is through "connectedness" that research ultimately is made authentic.

The scholarship of integration is, of course, closely related to discovery. It involves, first, doing research at the boundaries where fields converge, and it reveals itself in what philosopher-physicist Michael Polanyi calls "overlapping [academic] neighborhoods."[8] Such work is, in fact, increasingly important as traditional disciplinary categories prove confining, forcing new topologies of knowledge. Many of today's professors understand this. When we asked faculty to respond to the statement, "Multidisciplinary work is soft and should not be considered scholarship," only 8 percent agreed, 17 percent were neutral, while a striking 75 percent disagreed (table 1). This pattern of opinion, with only slight variation, was true for professors in all disciplines and across all types of institutions.

The scholarship of integration also means interpretation, fitting one's own research—or the research of others—into larger intellectual patterns. Such efforts are increasingly essential since specialization, without broader perspective, risks pedantry. The distinction we are drawing here between "discovery" and "integration" can be best understood, perhaps, by the questions posed. Those engaged in discovery ask, "What is to be known, what is yet to be found?" Those engaged in integration ask, "What do the findings mean? Is it possible to interpret what's been discovered in ways that provide a larger, more comprehensive understanding?" Questions such as

TABLE 1. MULTIDISCIPLINARY WORK IS SOFT AND SHOULD NOT BE CONSIDERED SCHOLARSHIP

	Agree	Neutral	Disagree
All respondents	**8%**	**17%**	**75%**
Research	7	9	84
Doctorate-granting	6	13	80
Comprehensive	8	14	78
Liberal arts	8	16	77
Two-year	9	27	63

Source: The Carnegie Foundation for the Advancement of Teaching, 1989 National Survey of Faculty.

these call for the power of critical analysis and interpretation. They have a legitimacy of their own and if carefully pursued can lead the scholar from information to knowledge and even, perhaps, to wisdom.

Today, more than at any time in recent memory, researchers feel the need to move beyond traditional disciplinary boundaries, communicate with colleagues in other fields, and discover patterns that connect. Anthropologist Clifford Geertz, of the Institute for Advanced Study in Princeton, has gone so far as to describe these shifts as a fundamental "refiguration, ... a phenomenon general enough and distinctive enough to suggest that what we are seeing is not just another redrawing of the cultural map—the moving of a few disputed borders, the marking of some more picturesque mountain lakes—but an alteration of the principles of mapping. Something is happening," Geertz says, " to the way we think about the way we think."[9]

This is reflected, he observes, in

> philosophical inquiries looking like literary criticism (think of Stanley Cavell on Beckett or Thoreau, Sartre on Flaubert), scientific discussions looking like *belles lettres morceaux* (Lewis Thomas, Loren Eisley), baroque fantasies presented as deadpan empirical observations (Borges, Barthelme), histories that consist of equations and tables or law court testimony (Fogel and Engerman, Le Roi Ladurie), documentaries that read like true confessions (Mailer), parables posing as ethnographies (Castaneda), theoretical treatises set out as travelogues (Levi-Strauss), ideological arguments cast as historiographical inquiries (Edward Said), epistemological studies constructed like political tracts (Paul Feyerabend), methodological polemics got up as personal memoirs (James Watson).[10]

These examples illustrate a variety of scholarly *trends—interdisciplinary, interpretive, integrative.* But we present them here as evidence that an intellectual sea change may be occurring, one that is perhaps as momentous as the nineteenth-century shift in the hierarchy of knowledge, when philosophy gave way more firmly to science. Today, interdisciplinary *and* integrative studies, long on the edges of academic life, are moving toward the center, responding both to new intellectual questions and to pressing human problems. As the boundaries of human knowledge are being dramatically reshaped, the academy surely must give increased attention to the *scholarship of integration.*

The Scholarship of Application

The first two kinds of scholarship—discovery and integration of knowledge—reflect the investigative and synthesizing traditions of academic life. The third element, the *application* of knowledge, moves toward engagement as the scholar asks, "How can knowledge be responsibly applied to consequential problems? How can it be helpful to individuals as well as institutions?" And further, "Can social problems *themselves* define an agenda for scholarly investigation?"

Reflecting the *Zeitgeist* of the nineteenth and early twentieth centuries, not only the land-grant colleges but also institutions such as Rensselaer Polytechnic Institute and the University of Chicago were founded on the principle that higher education must serve the interests of the larger community. In 1906, an editor celebrating the leadership of William Rainey Harper at the new University of Chicago defined what he believed to be the essential character of the American scholar. Scholarship, he observed, was regarded by the British as "a means and measure of self-development," by the Germans as "an end in itself," but by Americans as "equipment for service."[11] Self-serving though it may have been, this analysis had more than a grain of truth.

Given this tradition, one is struck by the gap between values in the academy and the needs of the larger world. Service is routinely praised, but accorded little attention—even in programs where it is most appropriate. Christopher Jencks and David Riesman, for example, have pointed out that when free-standing professional schools affiliated with universities, they lessened their commitment to applied work even though the original purpose of such schools was to connect theory and practice. Professional schools, they concluded, have oddly enough fostered "a more academic and less practical view of what their students need to know."[12]

Colleges and universities have recently rejected service as serious scholarship, partly because its meaning is so vague and often disconnected from serious intellectual work. As used today, service in the academy covers an almost endless number of campus activities—sitting on committees, advising student clubs, or performing departmental chores. The definition blurs still more as activities beyond the campus are included—participation in town councils, youth clubs, and the like. It is not unusual for almost any worthy project to be dumped into the amorphous category called "service."

Clearly, a sharp distinction must be drawn between *citizenship* activities and projects that relate to scholarship itself. To be sure, there are meritorious social and civic functions to be performed, and faculty should be appropriately recognized for such work. But all too frequently, service means not doing scholarship but doing good. To be considered *scholarship,* service activities must be tied directly to one's special field of knowledge and relate to, and flow directly out of, this professional activity. Such service is serious, demanding work, requiting the rigor—and the accountability—traditionally associated with research activities.

The *scholarship of application,* as we define it here, is not a one-way street. Indeed, the term itself may be misleading if it suggests that knowledge is first "discovered" and then "applied." The process we have in mind is far more dynamic. New intellectual understandings can arise out of the very act of application—whether in medical diagnosis, serving clients in psychotherapy, shaping public policy, creating an architectural design, or working with the public schools. In activities such as these, theory and practice vitally interact, and one renews the other.

Such a view of scholarly service—one that both applies and contributes to human knowledge is particularly needed in a world in which huge, almost intractable problems call for the skills and insights only the academy can provide. As Oscar Handlin observed, our troubled planet "can no longer afford the luxury of pursuits confined to an ivory tower.... [S]cholarship has to prove its worth not on its own terms but by service to the nation and the world."[13]

The Scholarship of Teaching

Finally, we come to the *scholarship of teaching.* The work of the professor becomes consequential only as it is understood by others. Yet, today, teaching is often viewed as a routine function, tacked on, something almost anyone can do. When defined as *scholarship,* however, teaching both educates and entices future scholars. Indeed, as Aristotle said, "Teaching is the highest form of understanding."

As a *scholarly* enterprise, teaching begins with what the teacher knows. Those who teach must, above all, be well informed, and steeped in the knowledge of their fields. Teaching can be well regarded only as professors are widely read and intellectually engaged. One reason legislators, trustees, and the general public often fail to understand why ten or twelve hours in the classroom each week can be a heavy load is their lack of awareness of the hard work and the serious study that undergirds good teaching.

Teaching is also a dynamic endeavor involving all the analogies, metaphors, and images that build bridges between the teacher's understanding and the student's learning. Pedagogical procedures must be carefully planned, continuously examined, and relate directly to the subject taught. Educator Parker Palmer strikes precisely the right note when he says knowing and learning are communal acts.[14] With this vision, great teachers create a common ground of intellectual commitment. They stimulate active, not passive, learning and encourage students to be critical, creative thinkers, with the capacity to go on learning after their college days are over.

Further, good teaching means that faculty, as scholars, are also learners. All too often, teachers transmit information that students are expected to memorize and then, perhaps, recall. While well-prepared lectures surely have a place, teaching, at its best, means not only *transmitting* knowledge, but *transforming* and *extending* it as well. Through reading, through classroom discussion, and surely through comments and questions posed by students, professors themselves will be pushed in creative new directions.

In the end, inspired teaching keeps the flame of scholarship alive. Almost all successful academics give credit to creative teachers—those mentors who defined their work so compellingly that it became, for them, a lifetime challenge. Without the teaching function, the continuity of knowledge will be broken and the store of human knowledge dangerously diminished.

Physicist Robert Oppenheimer, in a lecture at the two-hundredth anniversary of Columbia University in 1954, spoke elegantly of the teacher as mentor and placed teaching at the very heart of the scholarly endeavor: "The specialization of science is an inevitable accompaniment of progress; yet it is full of dangers, and it is cruelly wasteful, since so much that is beautiful and enlightening is cut off from most of the world. Thus it is proper to the role of the scientist that he not merely find the truth and communicate it to his fellows, but that he teach, that he try to bring the most honest and most intelligible account of new knowledge to all who will try to learn."[15]

Here, then, is our conclusion. What we urgently need today is a more inclusive view of what it means to be a scholar—a recognition that knowledge is acquired through research, through synthesis, through practice, and through teaching.[16] We acknowledge that these four categories—the scholarship of discovery, of integration, of application, and of teaching—divide intellectual functions that are tied inseparably to each other. Still, there is value, we believe, in analyzing the various kinds of academic work, while also acknowledging that they dynamically interact, forming an interdependent whole. Such a vision of scholarship, one that recognizes the great diversity of talent within the professoriate, also may prove especially useful to faculty as they reflect on the meaning and direction of their professional lives.

THE FACULTY

A Mosaic of Talent

The richness of faculty talent should be celebrated, not restricted. Only as the distinctiveness of each professor is affirmed will the potential of scholarship be fully realized. Surely, American higher education is imaginative and creative enough to support and reward not only those scholars uniquely gifted in research but also those who excel in the integration and application of knowledge, as well as those especially adept in the scholarship of teaching. Such a mosaic of talent, if acknowledged, would bring renewed vitality to higher learning and the nation.

While affirming the diversity of faculty functions, we wish also to underscore the point that some dimensions of scholarship are universal—mandates that apply to all.

First, all faculty should establish their credentials as *researchers.* Whether or not they choose specialized, investigative work on an ongoing basis, every scholar must, we believe, demonstrate the capacity to do original research, study a serious intellectual problem, and present to colleagues the results. Indeed, this is what the dissertation, or a comparable piece of creative work, is all about.

Second, all members of the faculty should, throughout their professional careers, stay in touch with developments in their fields and remain professionally alive. But we also underscore the point that this might be accomplished in different ways. As things now stand, "staying in touch" usually means launching new research projects and publishing on a regular basis. Such a pattern of productivity may fit the work of some professors. But it is unrealistic, we believe, to expect all faculty members, regardless of their interests, to engage in research and to publish on a regular timetable. For most scholars, creativity simply doesn't work that way.

We propose an alternative approach. Why not assume that staying in touch with one's field means just that—reading the literature and keeping well informed about consequential trends and patterns? Why not ask professors periodically to select the two or three most important new developments or significant new articles in their fields and then present, in writing, the reasons for their choices? Such a paper, one that could be peer reviewed, surely would help reveal the extent to which a faculty member is conversant with developments in his or her discipline, and is, in fact, remaining intellectually alive.

As a third mandate, every faculty member must be held to the highest standards of integrity. It goes without saying that plagiarism, the manipulation of laboratory data, the misuse of human or animal subjects in research, or any other form of deceptive or unethical behavior not only discredits the work of professors but also erodes the very foundation of the academy itself. Issues of professional integrity also arise in more subtle ways regarding teaching. For example, how well do faculty prepare for classroom presentation and how much advice and consultation do they give students outside the classroom?

Fourth, the work of the professoriate—regardless of the form it takes—must be carefully assessed. Excellence is the yardstick by which all scholarship must be measured. Effective ways surely must be found to evaluate faculty performance in the four dimensions of scholarship we discuss in this report, as difficult as the process may be. Faculty who engage in research, in teaching, in service, or in integrative work must demonstrate to the satisfaction of peers that high performance standards have been met.

Yet, today, at most four-year institutions, the requirements of tenure and promotion continue to focus heavily on research and on articles published in journals, especially those that are refereed (table 1). Good teaching is expected, but it is often inadequately assessed. And the category of "service," while given token recognition by most colleges, is consistently underrated, too.

In preparing this report, we conducted extensive conversations about standards for tenure and promotion with distinguished scholars and leaders of learned societies in five disciplines: chemistry, English,

TABLE 1. PERCENT OF FACULTY RATING THE FOLLOWING "VERY IMPORTANT" FOR GRANTING TENURE IN THEIR DEPARTMENT

	Research	Doctorate-Granting	Comprehensive	Liberal Arts	Two-Year
Number of publications	56%	55%	30%	8%	2%
Recommendations from outside scholars	53	29	9	16	3
Research grants received by the scholar	40	35	19	9	3
Reputations of presses or journals publishing the books or articles	40	32	18	7	2
Recommendations from other faculty within my institution	15	13	19	38	15
Student evaluations of courses taught	10	19	37	45	29
Lectures or papers delivered at professional meetings or at other colleges and universities	8	8	12	7	3
Published reviews of the scholar's books	8	7	5	3	1
Service within the scholar's discipline	6	8	13	11	7
Observations of teaching by colleagues and/or administrators	4	6	20	29	43
Service within the university community	3	6	17	27	19
Recommendations from current or former students	3	6	13	30	15
Academic advisement	1	2	6	15	6
Syllabi for courses taught	1	2	9	14	18

Source: The Carnegie Foundation for the Advancement of Teaching, 1989 National Survey of Faculty.

communications, economics, and business. We asked: Where in the United States are scholars in your field experimenting with alternative approaches to evaluation? These academics told us they know of few truly creative examples of faculty evaluation[s] that go beyond research and publication.

Richard Miller's survey of chief academic officers reinforced the point that the shift toward research has, in fact, been increasing at the expense of teaching. When asked how the balance [among] teaching, research, and service had shifted in recent years, only 5 percent reported that, at their institution, the move had been toward teaching, while 26 percent reported a shift toward research, away from teaching. This trend was especially striking at doctoral institutions, where 56 percent of the academic officers reported a move toward research and away from teaching and service (table 2).

One reason research and publication loom so large is that published articles are relatively easy to measure, at least quantitatively. There is, in most disciplines, a fairly clear hierarchy of journals and a recognized process of peer review. Books also are used for evaluation, although practice here varies from one discipline to another. For example, a department chairman at a ranking research university reported that "in psychology, all that counts is articles in high prestige journals. Even books don't count as much." Another scholar stated: "Economists have carefully studied publications and have developed a rank order for them. At research institutions, one must publish in particular journals. Quantitative studies are better than qualitative studies." Another scholar told our researcher, "Books are more important than articles at the Harvard Business School. And the book must get good reviews."[1] What's important, regardless of the field, is that research results must be published and peer reviewed.

But there is an irony in all of this. While journal articles—and occasionally books—are widely used to measure faculty performance, a strong undercurrent of dissatisfaction exists within the prevailing system. For example, more than 60 percent of today's faculty feel that teaching effectiveness, not publication, should be the *primary* criterion for promotion. While professors at two-year colleges feel most strongly about this, we found that 21 percent of those at research universities also support the proposition (table 3). Everett Ladd, of the University of Connecticut, captured the climate succinctly when he wrote that today's dominant emphasis on publication "is seriously out of touch with what [the faculty members] actually do and want to do."[2]

TABLE 2. HAS THE BALANCE OF IMPORTANCE AMONG TEACHING, RESEARCH, AND SERVICE AT YOUR INSTITUTION SHIFTED IN RECENT YEARS?

	All Respondents	Research	Doctorate-Granting	Comprehensive	Liberal Arts
Toward teaching, away from research and service	5%	13%	0%	1%	8%
Toward research, away from teaching and service	26	23	56	34	12
Toward service, away from teaching and research	1	3	0	1	0
Toward teaching and research, away from service	17	13	21	18	15
Toward research and service, away from teaching	5	7	3	8	2
Toward service and teaching, away from research	5	3	0	3	8
There has been no appreciable change.	39	33	21	31	51
Some other shift among teaching, research, and service	4	3	0	5	3

Source: Richard I. Miller, Hongyu Chen, Jerome B. Hart, and Clyde B. Killian, "New Approaches to Faculty Evaluation-A Survey, Initial Report" (Athens, OH: submitted to the Carnegie Foundation for the Advancement of Teaching by Richard I. Miller, professor of higher education, Ohio University, September 4, 1990), 19.

Even more disturbing, many faculty are skeptical about the seriousness with which publications are reviewed—a concern that calls into question the very integrity of the process. In our national survey, more than one-third of the faculty agreed that, on their campuses, publications are "just counted, not qualitatively measured" (table 4). We find it especially significant that 42 percent of those at research centers agree with this statement. Half the faculty at community colleges are neutral on the

TABLE 3. TEACHING EFFECTIVENESS SHOULD BE THE PRIMARY CRITERION FOR PROMOTION OF FACULTY

	Agree	Neutral	Disagree
All respondents	**62%**	**7%**	**31%**
Research	21	9	70
Doctorate-granting	41	11	48
Comprehensive	68	8	24
Liberal arts	76	6	18
Two-year	92	3	4

Source: The Carnegie Foundation for the Advancement of Teaching, 1989 National Survey of Faculty.

TABLE 4. AT MY INSTITUTION, PUBLICATIONS USED FOR TENURE AND PROMOTION ARE JUST COUNTED, NOT QUALITATIVELY MEASURED

	Agree	Neutral	Disagree
All respondents	**38%**	**25%**	**37%**
Research	42	9	49
Doctorate-granting	53	10	38
Comprehensive	54	14	32
Liberal arts	33	27	41
Two-year	19	50	31

Source: The Carnegie Foundation for the Advancement of Teaching, 1989 National Survey of Faculty.

issue, but this reflects, we believe, the relatively low priority assigned to publications at these institutions. We recognize that these are the findings of an opinion poll; still it suggests a disturbing lack of confidence in the system if a significant percentage of faculty believe publications are not seriously assessed.

Many faculty were particularly critical in their written comments about this issue. In responding to our questionnaire, a professor of mathematics at a comprehensive university put it this way: "It is assumed that all faculty can teach, and hence that one doesn't need to spend a lot of time on it. Good teaching is assumed, not rewarded. The administrators and many faculty don't regard extra time spent with students as time well spent.

This is the most frustrating aspect of my work." A biology professor at a top research university also expressed concern: "Only a few institutions can maintain a quality research reputation and a quality instructional program. In most, one comes at the expense of the other, and I view this as a major component in the decline of educational quality."[3]

There is another problem about the current reward system today that deserves comment. Research dollars are in very short supply, and even when a proposal is approved through peer review, it often dies for lack of funding. Indeed, estimates are that in some fields the odds of getting an approved proposal funded are only one in ten. Thus what we have is a no-win situation. While faculty are *assigned* the classes to be taught, they are, at the same time, expected to "go hunting" for research funds—a process that can be frustrating and time consuming. Further, they are often not rewarded for teaching while being penalized if they fail to do research.

There is a related matter. All faculty are often held to the same standards, and yet research support differs dramatically from one discipline to another. Traditionally, the natural sciences are in the most favored position, but in some fields—the humanities and arts, for example—grant funds are limited or nonexistent. One professor told a Carnegie researcher, "At our university, everyone is expected to do conventional research. I'm in the arts and not only is there no money for research, but the entire process seems oddly out-of-place with how quality in my field is and should be measured."[4]

Given these conditions, it's not surprising that most professors support the proposition that changes in faculty evaluation procedures are important and overdue. When we asked faculty to respond to the proposition, "At my institution we need better ways, besides publications, to evaluate the scholarly performance of the faculty," 68 percent agreed. Those at research and doctorate institutions, where current evaluation procedures seem most related to campus mission, also supported strongly the proposition. Faculty who feel least strongly about the need for change are those at two-year colleges, but, again, these are institutions that rely least on publications. Note especially that professors at comprehensive colleges and universities feel most strongly about the need for change (table 5).

We conclude that the full range of faculty talent must be more creatively assessed. It is unacceptable, we believe, to go on using research and publication as the primary criterion for tenure and promotion when other educational obligations are required. Further, it's administratively

TABLE 5. AT MY INSTITUTION WE NEED BETTER WAYS, BESIDES PUBLICATIONS, TO EVALUATE THE SCHOLARLY PERFORMANCE OF THE FACULTY

	Agree	Neutral	Disagree
All respondents	**68%**	**19%**	**13%**
Research	69	12	19
Doctorate-granting	77	10	14
Comprehensive	80	11	10
Liberal arts	69	16	15
Two-year	55	33	12

Source: The Carnegie Foundation for the Advancement of Teaching, 1989 National Survey of Faculty.

unwise to ignore the fact that a significant number of faculty are dissatisfied with the current system. Even more important, it is inappropriate to use evaluation procedures that restrict faculty, distort institutional priorities, and neglect the needs of students. Clearly, the time has come not only to reconsider the meaning of scholarship but also to take the next step and consider ways by which the faculty reward system can be improved.

But what options should be considered? How can the reward system become more flexible and more vital, evaluating faculty performance beyond the scholarship of discovery?

As a first step, we urge that faculty assessment take into account a broader range of writing, especially in advancing the scholarship of integration. While articles in refereed journals and scholarly books are of great value, writing a textbook also can be a significant intellectual endeavor. Of course, textbooks, like journal articles, differ greatly in quality and must be evaluated as rigorously as any other form of scholarly work. Still, such writing, if well done, can reveal a professor's knowledge of the field, illuminate essential integrative themes, and powerfully contribute to excellence in teaching, too.

Writing for nonspecialists—often called "popular writing"—also should be recognized as a legitimate scholarly endeavor. In the past, such work has frequently been dismissed as "mere journalism," but this misses, we believe, a larger point. To make complex ideas understandable to a large audience can be a difficult, demanding task, one that requires not only a deep and thorough knowledge of one's field but keen literary skills, as well. Such effort, when successful, surely should be recognized and rewarded. The writings of Stephen Jay Gould in *Natural History*, the essays of Lewis Thomas, and Stephen Hawking's brilliant little book on the history of time illustrate, at the highest level, the kinds of contributions we have in mind.

Developing the right standards and finding qualified peers to review articles in nonacademic publications may be difficult, but still it is important. As a first step, it seems reasonable to assume that scholars who, themselves, have written for a wider audience will understand the importance, as well as the difficulty, of the process, making them appropriate peer reviewers. We remain convinced that these broader forms of communication merit serious consideration, and those evaluating such scholarship might ask: Does the work show a careful understanding of the discipline? Have key issues been well defined and creative insights well presented? Has the essential message been clarified? In what ways has public discourse been advanced?

Let's also acknowledge that scholarship often finds expression in other ways as well. Preparing quality computer software, for example, is increasingly a function of serious scholars, and even videocassette and television offer opportunity for communicating ideas to nonspecialists in creative new ways. This potential was used by Jacob Bronowski, the British scholar, in his series "The Ascent of Man," which was broadcast on American public television in the early 1970s—a presentation of Western intellectual history in which Bronowski, educated as a mathematician, could extend brilliantly his insightful talents as a poet, inventor, and playwright.

Designing new courses and participating in curricular innovations are examples of yet another type of professional work deserving recognition. Those who help shape a core curriculum or prepare a cross-disciplinary seminar surely are engaged in the scholarship of *integration*, and, again, such activity should be acknowledged and rewarded. In evaluating scholarship of this sort, key questions should be asked: Have course objectives been well defined? Has the relevant literature been cited and integrated in the course? Are key points covered and appropriate thematic relationships made?

What about *applied* scholarship? Today, almost all colleges and universities say faculty should engage in teaching, research, and service, but when it comes to tenure and promotion, [service] often is forgotten. Since such oversight restricts both the utility and the creativity of higher education, ways must be found to [en]sure that professional service is taken seriously. Means are needed to document such activity and then evaluate it. We stress again, however, that service is not a "catch-all" category.

While social and civic projects are important, they should not be considered a part of the scholarship of application. What should be included are activities that relate directly to the intellectual work of the professor and carried out through consultation, technical assistance, policy analysis, program evaluation, and the like.

In documenting *applied* work—of whatever form—faculty should include not only their own written record of the project but also the evaluations of those who received the service. Further, since applied work may take place beyond the campus, outside experts might be asked to sit on review committees. Those assessing applied scholarship should ask: Is the activity directly related to the academic expertise of the professor? Have project goals been defined, procedures well planned, and actions carefully recorded? In what ways has the work not only benefited the recipients of such activity but also added to the professor's own understanding of his or her academic field?

The question of how to evaluate *teaching* remains a mare's nest of controversy. The problem relates not only to procedures but also to the weight assigned to the endeavor. Teaching, as presently viewed, is like a currency that has value in its own country but can't be converted into other currencies. It may be highly regarded on a sizeable campus and yet not be a particularly marketable skill. Thus, for faculty members whose primary loyalty is to their careers rather than to their institutions, teaching now counts little in increasing prospects to move on and move up. Consequently, excellence in the classroom all too often is undervalued.

For teaching to be considered equal to research, it must be vigorously assessed, using criteria that we recognized within the academy, not just in a single institution. But what might such an institution look like? Whose opinions should be used?

As openers, we suggest that evidence to assess faculty be gathered from at least three sources: self-assessment, peer assessment, and student assessment. As to self-evaluation, it seems appropriate to ask faculty, periodically, to prepare a statement about the courses taught—one that includes a discussion of class goals and procedures, course outlines, descriptions of teaching materials and assignments, and copies of examinations or other evaluation tasks. Faculty might also be asked to step back and discuss, more informally, their impressions about the gains and losses experienced in the classroom—what worked well, what barriers were encountered, what steps might be taken to improve the course next time around.

Then there is peer evaluation. In our survey of academic leaders, we found ambivalence about peer review, a method which may be accepted in theory but neglected in practice. Granted, a communications professor at one ranking university told a Carnegie researcher: "There is peer review of teaching on our campus, since we believe there is a strong connection between scholarship and teaching," but this was an exception. A professor at a large state university reported: "The faculty here are opposed to peer review of teaching. The union contract will not allow it." And a faculty member at a land-grant university said: "As department chairman I attempted peer review, but the faculty voted against it after two years because it was too time consuming."[5]

Problems notwithstanding, faculty should, we believe, be primarily responsible for evaluating the teaching performance of colleagues, and the process should be as systematic as that used to evaluate research. Criteria for such assessment should be defined, and data-gathering procedures carefully developed. Specifically, faculty might work together to establish criteria for good teaching, be encouraged to move freely in and out of classrooms, observing colleagues and discussing their own teaching procedures. In addition, a faculty member might be asked to submit an essay on his or her own philosophy of teaching. Such a statement could highlight the theoretical assumptions that undergird that faculty member's teaching procedures and help not only the reviewer but the candidate as well.

Northwestern State University in Louisiana recently introduced a new faculty program called "Teaching Circles"—groups of five to seven faculty who voluntarily come together, with one member designated as leader. The goal is to focus exclusively on teaching. Those participating observe each other's teaching and together review classroom events. The assumption is that awareness about good practice will improve as faculty meet in small groups—on an ongoing basis—to discuss pedagogical procedures. In such a process, peer evaluation will be more readily embraced.[6]

Peer review might take yet another form. A distinguished professor told one of our researchers that, at his institution, a faculty member's commitment to and insight about good teaching are evaluated through journals that focus specifically on teaching. "In my own field of chemistry," he said, "the *Journal of Chemical Education* is used as a forum for those who wish to report on good teaching practice, and the journal is widely read."[7] Articles about teaching should be peer reviewed and given weight for tenure and promotion. In addition, national associations increasingly are including teaching as an agenda topic at their conventions. Papers prepared and presented at such sessions also merit consideration. Regardless of the method used, we urge a serious, systematic approach to the evaluation of teaching by one's colleagues.

Students also have a role to play. Although negative voices were sometimes heard, most of the scholars we interviewed spoke favorably of involving students in evaluation. A professor at one of the nation's most prestigious institutions reported: "At our university teaching is increasingly important. Faculty can, in fact, choose a teaching track. We have student evaluations and interviews with students as part of the year-to-year and tenure process." Another reported: "Faculty at our university read course syllabi and also student evaluations are seriously considered." A professor at MIT told us, "Our business students are intolerant of bad teaching. Student evaluations play a role in faculty assessment and all tenured faculty share in the review."[8]

The benefits of student evaluation were captured recently in a letter to *The Chronicle of Higher Education.* Mary Ellen Elwell, professor at Salisbury State University, wrote:

> After 20 years of undergraduate teaching with careful attention to a variety of evaluation instruments completed by my students, I am convinced that I have improved by working on the inadequacies identified by students. While I am grateful that my academic future has not rested solely on these often-flawed instruments and their sometimes strange statistical manipulation, I value my students' assessment. In my experience, they have generally been more perceptive than I anticipate and more generous than I deserve.[9]

Again, we urge that student evaluation be used in making decisions about tenure and promotion. But for this to work, procedures must be well designed and students must be well prepared. It's a mistake to ask students to fill out a form at the end of a class without a serious consideration of the process. Specifically, we urge that a session on faculty assessment be part of freshman orientation. All incoming students should discuss the importance of the process and the procedures used. Students also should be asked how teacher evaluation can be improved. Such involvement would help undergraduates think carefully about good teaching—and improve their assessment, too.

Some faculty insist the true value of a class can be judged best only over time. For this reason, we suggest asking *former* students to help with evaluation, especially in tenure decisions. Bowdoin College, for example, sends a written form to graduates, asking them to evaluate former teachers. Skidmore College, along with many other institutions, has also successfully introduced procedures for contacting alumni—especially in tenure cases—to gain retrospective assessments. In the end, all evaluators of teaching should ask: Have class goals been well defined? Is the content up-to-date? Do instructional procedures strike a balance between faculty leadership and student initiative? Are the methods of assessment adequate? And has the teacher been informed and enriched as a result of the experience?

Throughout this chapter, we have stressed the importance of written documentation in evaluating faculty performance of putting evidence down on paper. However, professional performance can and should be judged in other ways as well. For example, artistic endeavors such as music recitals and performances, juried exhibitions of art work, and theatrical and dance productions also must be carefully critiqued by specialists. In preparing for such evaluation, we urge that scholars in these fields provide tapes, photographs, videocassettes, and perhaps also describe in writing, their creative process—not only interpreting their own work but [also] comparing it to the works of others, placing it in perspective.

When it comes to pulling all the evidence together, we are impressed by the *portfolio* idea—a procedure that encourages faculty to document their work in a variety of ways. A faculty member could choose the form of scholarship around which a portfolio might be developed. The material used could include many of the varied forms we've described—ranging from publications, to field work documentation, to course descriptions, peer reviews, student evaluations, and even, perhaps, recordings and videocassettes.

Above all, faculty evaluation should be not only systematic but flexible as well. While all colleges should have well-defined procedures, each faculty member also should play a central role in shaping the criteria to be used in his or her evaluation. Recently, all departments at Syracuse University were asked to review promotion and tenure guidelines and define creative new standards. The Writing Program was the first to respond. Candidates in this program are now to be evaluated in ways that cut across traditional categories of teaching, research, and service. For example, the guidelines speak of significant intellectual work by faculty that includes such activity as "creating new knowledge," "connecting knowledge to other knowledge," "making specialized knowledge publicly accessible and usable," and "communicating ... experience through artistic works or performance."[10] Within these broad categories, the rich diversity of scholarship is encouraged.

Kenneth E. Eble, of the University of Utah, in capturing this spirit, urged that faculty "seek to broaden definitions of professional competence and humanize the means by which we arrive at such judgments." He went on to offer some useful prescriptions: "Put less stress on evaluating what we have done and more on stimulating what we might do. Do less counting of our own and our colleagues' publications and more thinking about what we do day-to-day which will never be published. Do less longing to arrive at the higher goals of academe and more about making wherever you are a livable and interesting and compassionate community."[11] Where such conditions exist, the wide range of faculty talent will be tapped, students will be well served, and scholarship, in a richer, fuller sense, will be affirmed.

THE CREATIVITY CONTRACT

The quality of scholarship is dependent, above all else, on the vitality of each professor. Colleges and universities that flourish help faculty build on their strengths and sustain their own creative energies, throughout a lifetime. Henry David Thoreau captured the importance of such renewal in commenting on his decision to leave the solitary, reflective life at Walden Pond. "I left the woods," he wrote, "for as good a reason as I went there ... it seemed to me that I had several more lives to lead, and could not spare any more time for that one. It is remarkable how easily and insensibly we fall into a particular route, and make a beaten track for ourselves."[1]

It flies in the face of all experience to expect a professor to engage in the same type of performance across an entire career, without a change of pace. Faculty renewal is essential. Yet, today, academic work is defined, all too frequently, in single-dimensional terms, with research and publications used as the yardstick by which success is measured. In such a climate, those who don't publish with regularity are often considered "deadwood," as if professional commitments are narrow and unchanging. Such a suffocatingly restricted view of scholarship leads frequently to burnout or plateaus of performance as faculty are expected to do essentially the same things, year after year.

The irony is that most professors do not think of themselves simply as researchers. Even a quarter of a century ago, studies revealed that while faculty identified strongly with their own disciplines, they also wanted teaching to be more highly valued. More recently, data from the 1989 Carnegie Foundation faculty survey show that for 70 percent of today's professors, teaching represents their primary interest (table 1). And it's equally significant, we believe, that even at research universities, about one-third of the faculty support this proposition, while at two-year institutions it was 93 percent. Faculty may not view research as their preferred function and yet, year after year, they are often held to this single measure of success.

To counter burnout or stagnation, scholarship in its fullest sense must be acknowledged. This means not only broadening the reward system but also creating flexible and varied career paths for professors. We urgently need arrangements that encourage shifts and alterations throughout a lifetime. Lee Knefelkamp, of Columbia University, captured elegantly the professional pattern we have in mind when she urged that academic life be viewed through the metaphor of "seasons." Knefelkamp writes that faculty members may, in fact, change their interests, "revisit tasks, challenges, phases, stages—seasons—dozens of times during our academic careers. There is no rhythm that fits every single person ..."[2]

Underlying such rhythms are forces deeply rooted in the life pattern of every individual. Roger Baldwin and Robert Blackburn, citing the work of psychologist Daniel Levinson, describe adulthood as having stable and transitional periods. "During the stable periods the adult pursues fairly clear goals. But periodically, the individual must reorder priorities and change behavior in order to compensate for neglected dimensions of the

TABLE 1. DO YOUR INTERESTS LIE PRIMARILY IN RESEARCH OR IN TEACHING?

	Research	Teaching
All respondents	**30%**	**70%**
Research	66	33
Doctorate-granting	45	55
Comprehensive	23	77
Liberal arts	17	83
Two-year	7	93

Source: The Carnegie Foundation for the Advancement of Teaching,1989 National Survey of Faculty.

self (e.g., unfulfilled ambitions, newly acquired interests)."[3] Erik Erikson, approaching life patterns from yet another perspective, describes the middle years of adulthood as a time when "generativity" and "stagnation" are in competition. Generativity, Erikson points out, is sparked by new priorities, a larger sense of caring, a desire to reach out, to share and belong. Stagnation, on the other hand, results from feelings of isolation, a belief that one's work has little meaning.[4]

Members of the professoriate also experience periods of stability and change. But for faculty, such ebbs and flows are profoundly influenced—and complicated—by professionally imposed hurdles. The novice instructor, for example, is expected to master new skills and gain full entry into the academic world. In today's marketplace, this may mean spending several years as a "gypsy scholar," moving from campus to campus on one-year or part-time appointments. Facing profound uncertainty, the young academic still is expected to teach and publish articles and books. Further, new faculty may find career pressures competing with family obligations—a situation compounded by the trend toward longer post-doctoral work in many fields.

Faculty who *do* secure a tenure-track position often are obliged to publish with regularity and "make a name" for themselves. But this is also a season when teaching can be especially time consuming, when professors are expected to do departmental chores and serve on campuswide committees. The danger is stress and burnout, and in our faculty survey, 53 percent of those under forty years of age reported that "my job is a source of considerable personal strain." It's also true, however, that pressure declines as experience increases (table 2).

TABLE 2. MY JOB IS THE SOURCE OF CONSIDERABLE PERSONAL STRAIN

	Agree	Neutral	Disagree
All faculty	**44%**	**11%**	**45%**
Age			
Under 40	53	13	34
40 to 49	44	11	45
50 to 59	41	9	50
60 to 64	41	12	57
65 and over	26	9	64

Source: The Carnegie Foundation for the Advancement of Teaching, *The Condition of the Professoriate: Attitudes and Trends* (1989), 82.

Significantly, younger faculty believe that the quality of their work is, in fact, diminished by competing obligations. More than half of those we surveyed stated that, "I hardly ever get time to give a piece of work the attention it deserves"; while less than one-third of the faculty over sixty have this concern (table 3). In addition, 43 percent of faculty under forty fear that the "pressure to publish reduces the quality of teaching at my university" (table 4).

Roger G. Baldwin, in commenting on pressures of the professoriate, notes that "the press of fixed responsibilities leaves little time to stay broadly informed of developments in one's field or to plan for an uncertain future.... Keeping the demands of the early career manageable

TABLE 3. I HARDLY EVER GET TIME TO GIVE A PIECE OF WORK THE ATTENTION IT DESERVES

	Agree	Neutral	Disagree
All faculty	**43%**	**13%**	**44%**
Age			
Under 40	53	13	34
40 to 49	49	13	39
50 to 59	38	14	48
60 to 64	33	14	53
65 and over	29	11	60

Source: The Carnegie Foundation for the Advancement of Teaching, *The Condition of the Professoriate: Attitudes and Trends* (1989), 81.

TABLE 4. THE PRESSURE TO PUBLISH REDUCES THE QUALITY OF TEACHING AT MY UNIVERSITY

	Agree	Neutral	Disagree
All faculty	**35%**	**19%**	**46%**
Age			
Under 40	43	20	37
40 to 49	34	18	48
50 to 59	32	18	50
60 to 64	31	25	45
65 and over	39	21	40

Source: The Carnegie Foundation for the Advancement of Teaching, *The Condition of the Professoriate: Attitudes and Trends* (1989), 51.

can prevent burnout and preserve fragile faculty morale."[5] Late-career professors march to different drummers. Faculty, in this season, if they are successful, experience a peak in status and recognition, and demands for their service from outside their institution often grow. Psychologist Wilbert J. McKeachie, at the University of Michigan, comments: "For the established senior professor, service on national committees, requests to write chapters in invited symposia, or invitations to deliver addresses may take time formerly devoted to research and teaching."[6] However, for most faculty at this stage—those not in leadership positions—the principal danger is becoming stuck on a "career plateau."

At the far end of the spectrum, older professors also need new challenges if they are to avoid the worst hazards of disengagement—feeling isolated from disciplinary developments and irrelevant to institutional concerns. What is most certain, and must be more fully recognized, is that faculty in late career stages still have considerable capacity for growth. Given their great breadth of knowledge and experience, such individuals are prime candidates for integrative and applied scholarship, for example. And as experienced teachers, they can be especially helpful to younger faculty. Career paths for senior professors should be more flexible and varied.

The argument for career flexibility relates also to variations in the disciplines, since patterns of productivity appear to vary from field to field. Mathematicians and physicists, for example, are most productive in their younger years, while historians and philosophers tend to be most productive later on. Einstein propounded his special theory of relativity at age of twenty-six, while Kant's seminal work, *The Critique of Pure Reason,* did not appear until he was fifty-seven, and then, for the next nine years, he followed with an outpouring of writings that revolutionized philosophical thought.

Recently, the *Washington Post* presented graphs showing the varying patterns of outstanding contributions over lifetimes. Physicists, for example, make most of their contributions by age thirty-five, with astronomers peaking about ten years later. In the arts, lyric poets hit peak creativity before age thirty, while novelists mature somewhat later, reaching the height of their creative powers around age forty-five (figure 1). It is particularly heartening to note that in some fields creativity that has declined surges again in late life. Any system of faculty evaluation and reward should, we believe, recognize the differing patterns of productivity in faculty, so far as age, career, and the discipline are concerned.

FIGURE 1. THE HEIGHT OF CREATIVE POWERS

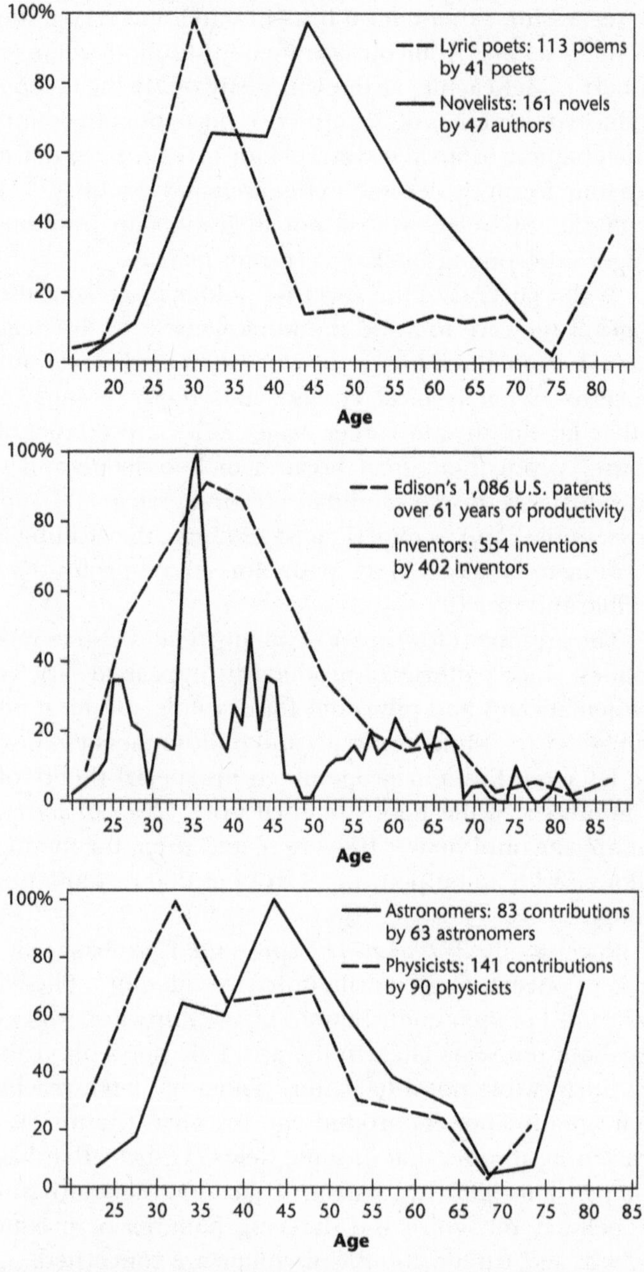

Source: Malcolm Gladwell, "Why, In Some Fields, Do Early Achievers Seem to Be the Only Kind?" *Washington Post* (April 16, 1990), Final Edition, A3.

Given personal and professional changes that occur across a lifetime, what's needed, we believe, are career paths that provide for flexibility and change. Alternating periods of goal seeking and reassessment should be common for all academics. As Roger Baldwin writes, "Higher education should acknowledge the changing character of these periods and help professors travel through them successfully."[7] Specifically, we recommend that colleges and universities develop what might be called "creativity contracts"—an arrangement by which faculty members define their professional goals for a three- to five-year period, possibly shifting from one principal scholarly focus to another. Indeed, looking down the road, we can see the day when staying with one dimension of scholarship—without a break—would be considered the exception, not the rule.

Here's how the creativity contract might work: We can imagine a faculty member devoting most of his or her early career to specialized research. Then the scholar might wish to examine integrative questions—taking time to read in other fields, write interpretive essays or a textbook, or spend time with a mentor on another campus to discuss the implications of his or her work. Still later, the creativity contract might focus on an applied project, one that would involve the professor in school consultations or as an advisor to a governmental body. And a contract surely could, from time to time, focus on the scholarship of teaching. The professor might agree to revise a course, design a new one, or prepare new teaching materials, using videos or film segments, for example. All such activities should, of course, be well documented and carefully assessed.

What we propose, in short, is that faculty expectations and related evaluation not only be *broadened* but that they be *individualized and continuous* as well. If faculty are to build on their strengths and contribute constructively to the institutions where they work, evaluation criteria must be tailored to personal talents, as well as campus needs. And it is especially important, we believe, that the criteria used reflect changing patterns of personal and professional growth across a lifetime. Once again, *diversity*, not uniformity, is the key.

We are aware that many institutions already have informal arrangements for faculty professional growth. Georgia State University's College of Business Administration, for example, "has a new policy that allows professors to choose from five career 'profiles': a traditional profile, which places equal weight on research and teaching; a research profile; a teaching profile; a service profile; and an administrative profile. All five carry minimum expectations for teaching, research, and service."[8] Such efforts make it possible for faculty to interrupt their schedules to complete a degree program, take time for research and publication, work on teaching duties, and participate in national professional activities. We believe these practices could be the basis for what we have called the "creativity contract."

The potential benefit of a flexible career path was revealed in a comment we received from a senior professor at a research institution. "[A] few years ago," he said "I felt much differently about my work and institution than I do now. I would have answered your questions on morale and a career change negatively then. [But] my school gave me the time, room, and encouragement to move in new directions. In my case, I am now directing new writing programs campuswide and introducing new concepts like computer-assisted instruction in writing and writing across the curriculum. I have, quite frankly, felt a sense of renewed purpose, energy, and usefulness in my work. I hope that other institutions are as flexible and open to new ideas as mine."[9]

The creativity contract idea may appear utopian, but it is attainable, we believe. The goal is not to encourage an erratic pattern of activity; rather, it is to sustain productivity across a lifetime. Such a creativity contract, if appropriately designed, will acknowledge the diversity of talent, as well as the changing seasons of academic life and have the capacity to keep faculty creative and productive. These characteristics are essential if education is to be enriched and if the life of each professor [is to be] continually renewed.

THE CAMPUSES

Diversity with Dignity

Broadening scholarship has implications not only for individuals but for institutions, too. Today's higher education leaders speak with pride about the distinctive missions of their campuses. But such talk often masks a pattern of conformity. Too many campuses are inclined to seek status by imitating what they perceive to be more prestigious institutions. We are persuaded that if scholarship is to be enriched, every college and university must clarify its own goals and seek to relate its own unique purposes more directly to the reward system for professors.

In 1963, Clark Kerr, then president of the University of California, delivered his widely noted Godkin lectures in Cambridge, Massachusetts. He told the audience at Harvard University: "The university is being called upon to educate previously unimagined numbers of students; to respond to the expanding claims of national service; to merge its activities with industry as never before; to adapt to and rechannel new intellectual currents." Only when this transformation had taken place, Kerr predicted, would we have "a truly American university, an institution unique in world history, an institution not looking to other models but serving, itself, as a model for universities in other parts of the globe."[1]

This forecast has largely come to pass. A network of world-ranked research centers has been built. But we have done more: doctorate-granting institutions, liberal arts campuses, and a category called comprehensive colleges and universities [that] offer a truly remarkable range of programs. Beyond that, more than a thousand two-year and specialized institutions are scattered from coast to coast. This pattern, above all else, reflects a deep national commitment to open higher education to the broadest possible range of our citizenry. But even as the number of institutions grew, a single model of scholarship came to dominate the system, and the nation's higher learning institutions increasingly have become more *imitative than distinctive.*

As far back as 1956, David Riesman described the "snakelike procession" in which colleges and universities, especially the newer ones, tend to follow the path taken by older, more established institutions, reinforcing a practice that occasionally has been called the upward drift.[2] Rather than defining their *own* roles and confidently shaping their *own* distinctive missions, campuses increasingly seek to gain status by emulating research centers. Some changed their name; others simply changed the rules by which faculty are recruited or rewarded. Either way, many institutions have lost a sense of distinctiveness, and scholarship's potential has remained strikingly unfulfilled.

During the 1950s we had, in the United States, a network of colleges that took pride in their unique missions. Often referring to themselves as "experimental," these institutions were unusually creative in developing new curriculum designs, or in promoting work-study programs, or in innovative living-learning arrangements, or in assessing imaginatively the undergraduate program. Much of this excitement has diminished, and what we would like to see today are more colleges and universities that take pride in their uniqueness.

To be sure, no two colleges are alike. We have, in the United States, universities that focus largely on research. We have land-grant and urban colleges and universities that speak of public service, and our system of higher education has an impressive array of two-year and liberal arts colleges, as well, that know quite clearly what they are. Still, the tendency in recent years has been to impose a single model of scholarship on the entire higher education enterprise.

The power of this imitative pattern was vividly illustrated in a letter we recently received from a faculty member at a Midwest institution that, in just twenty years, had gone from a teachers' college to a "doctorate" institution. We were told that "now the goal is to gain a Research designation in the next decade." The professor writes: "Those hired during the doctoral period—most of the faculty—are now being required to change their priorities in order to be promoted, and the faculty being hired are radically different in orientation from many of their colleagues. Those who have been very service- or teaching-oriented for years are finding they cannot be promoted or receive merit pay in this new situation. Many are retiring early, and the union and administration are grappling with this transition."[3]

Simply stated, what we have on many campuses today is a crisis of purpose. Far too many colleges and universities are being driven not by self-defined objectives but by the external imperatives of prestige. Even institutions that enroll primarily undergraduates—and have few if any resources for research—seek to imitate ranking research centers. In the process, their mission becomes blurred, standards of research are compromised, and the quality of teaching and learning is disturbingly diminished. "By believing themselves to be what they are not…" as Ernest Lynton and Sandra Elman of the University of Massachusetts put it, "institutions fall short of being what they could be" and, in the process, not only deprive society of substantial intellectual services but also diminish the vitality of higher learning.[4]

The issue here is not whether an institution should be concerned about quality or status—or whether a campus mission might be changed. Rather, our concern is with the uniformity of the pattern and the divisive struggle on many campuses between "teaching" and "research." At some places the two functions can in fact fit easily together. In graduate seminars, for example, a clear connection often can be made between scholarly investigation and classroom instruction. At that level, faculty and student cultures intersect and, further, graduate faculty often have a very light teaching load to accommodate their research.

But at the undergraduate level, and most especially in general education courses, research work often competes with classroom obligations, both in time and content. Faculty assigned to teach such courses frequently must take shortcuts in their research or rely heavily on teaching assistants—an arrangement that is often less than satisfactory for both student and professor. We find it revealing, for example, that, in our surveys, more than half the faculty at research and doctorate institutions agreed that at their institution "the pressure to publish reduces the quality of teaching" (appendix [table] A.32).

In the push for external recognition, faculty teaching loads are reduced. At big universities, freshmen and sophomores often are assigned to large sections, meeting with "TAs." Undergraduates are especially frustrated when they find themselves trapped in a system where their own interests are put in second place. This adds up to the perception that many institutions are more concerned about status than about their students.

But ground rules may be changing. The heady days of rampant physical expansion in American higher education have long since faded. Faculty mobility has slowed, and rather than view their present position as a stepping stone to a more prestigious one, increased numbers of professors have dug deep roots. With the growing recognition that one's career might easily be spent at a single institution, loyalty to the local campus appears to be increasing. When the Carnegie Foundation surveyed faculty in 1984, only 29 percent said their college or university was "very important" to them. Last year, it was 40 percent (table 1).

Further, while the academic discipline is still important, faculty increasingly are expressing loyalty to the campus, and we are impressed that colleges and universities—even the big, complex ones—refer to the campus as a "community," and some even use the metaphor of "family." In 1989, when we surveyed several hundred college and university presidents, 96 percent said they "strongly believe in the importance of community." Almost all respondents also agreed that "community is appropriate for my campus" and supported the proposition that "administrators should make a greater effort to strengthen common purposes and shared experiences."[5]

We urge, then, that every higher learning institution define its own special mission and develop a system of faculty recognition that relates to what the campus is seeking to accomplish, and the four categories of scholarship discussed in this report could serve as a framework for such discussions. But beyond this basic mandate, some campuses might, for example, decide to give priority to research, others might elect to give special emphasis

TABLE 1. PERCENT OF FACULTY WHO RATE THE FOLLOWING "VERY IMPORTANT" TO THEM: 1984 AND 1989

	1984	1989
Their academic discipline	76%	77%
Their department	41	53
Their college or university	29	40

Source: The Carnegie Foundation for the Advancement of Teaching, 1984 and 1989 National Surveys of Faculty.

to teaching, while still others [emphasize] the integration or application of knowledge, and some may provide a blend of all. Each college or university should, of course, view teaching as a core requirement. We also can imagine that even *within* institutions, different priorities may prevail from one department or division to another. And even within *departments* there could be a "mosaic of talent." We're suggesting that diversity, not uniformity, be the goal, and in this spirit, we outline [in the following] possible options for the full range of colleges and universities in the nation.

At the *research university*, original research and publication should remain the basic expectations and be considered the key criteria by which the performance of most faculty will be assessed. Where else but in our major research universities—with their intellectual and physical resources and their tradition of rigorous and untrammeled inquiry—should the bulk of research in a free society be conducted and rewarded?

But at research centers, the integration and application of knowledge also should be valued. Interdisciplinary institutes, for example, provide a unique opportunity for scholars from different backgrounds to fit their specialized studies into larger intellectual patterns. At the same time, professional schools within the universities have the capacity to transform "in the nation's service" from a slogan to a reality.

Research universities also must aggressively support teaching. After all, a significant percentage of their students are undergraduates, and such institutions are clearly obligated to provide them a quality education. Is it ethical to enroll students and not give them the attention they deserve? Christopher Jencks and David Riesman, writing in 1968, vividly described the price that's paid when teaching is neglected: "No doubt most professors prefer it when their courses are popular, their lectures applauded, and their former students appreciative. But since such successes are of no help in getting a salary increase, moving to a more prestigious campus, or winning their colleagues' admiration, they are unlikely to struggle as hard to create them as to do other things. . . . Many potentially competent teachers do a conspicuously bad job in the classroom because they know that bad teaching is not penalized in any formal way."[6]

To expect faculty to be good teachers, as well as good researchers, is to set a demanding standard. Still, it is at the research university, more than any other, where the two must come together. To bring teaching and research into better balance, we urge the nation's ranking universities to extend special status and salary incentives to those professors who devote most of their time to teaching and are particularly effective in the classroom. Such recognition will signify that the campus regards teaching excellence as a hallmark of professional success.

At doctorate-granting universities a different approach to scholarship is needed. These institutions typically see themselves as being "in transition," embracing to a very large degree the research model. As an administrator at one such campus expressed it, "Our goal is to be in the top twenty or certainly in the top fifty."[7] Surely, research is central for *some* professors, and doctorate-granting institutions can take legitimate pride in the national and international reputations of such scholars. However, doctorate-granting institutions need also to recognize professors who make exceptional contributions to other scholarly areas: integration, application, and teaching. At these institutions, perhaps more than any others, the mosaic of talent should be carefully considered.

A president at a doctorate university, in commenting on the mission of his institution, put it this way: "This campus should be a place where both great teachers *and* great researchers function side by side.

"We should have the confidence to say, 'Look, you're a great researcher and we are eager to have you here doing what you do best.'" He then added, "We should also be able to say to a colleague, 'You are terrific with students, but you are not publishing. Still, we want you to help us perform an important mission on the campus.'"[8] This is precisely the kind of division of labor that should be clarified and strengthened at doctorate-granting institutions.

We are impressed by the service potential of doctorate universities, especially those located in large cities. For years, there has been talk of building a network of "urban-grant" institutions, modeled after the land-grant tradition. We support such a movement and urge these institutions to apply their resources creatively to problems of the city—to health care, education, municipal government, and the like. What we are suggesting is that many doctoral institutions have not just a national, but more important perhaps, a *regional* mission to fulfill, too, and faculty should be rewarded for participating in these more local endeavors.

Liberal arts colleges have, historically, taken pride in the scholarship of teaching. Faculty on these campuses frequently are hired with the understanding that spending time with students, both inside and outside the classroom, is of prime importance. It seems clear that teaching undergraduates should continue to be viewed as the measure of success for liberal arts colleges. And professors at these schools should be assured, in unequivocal terms, that rewards will be based heavily on such work.

But, here again, the position cannot be absolute. Liberal arts colleges provide an especially supportive climate for the scholarship of integration. On these campuses, there is, or should be, a climate of intellectual exchange that fosters interdisciplinary studies, creative general education courses, and capstone seminars. Kenneth Ruscio, in his study called "The Distinctive Scholarship of the Selective Liberal Arts College," has found that the work of academics in small colleges is, in fact, more "horizontal," reaching across disciplines and bringing together ideas from a variety of sources. Ruscio concludes that "the boundaries of specializations and the taxonomies of the disciplines are considered artificial and constraining."[9]

While teaching remains central at the liberal arts college, faculty members may, from time to time, choose to focus on a research project, at least at one point or another in their careers. And funds should be made available for such work. It is unacceptable to expect faculty to conduct consequential investigation and to publish without the time and resources to do the job. But we would particularly encourage faculty at liberal arts colleges to establish collaborative relationships with colleagues at research universities so that resources might be shared. Two groups of liberal arts colleges in the Midwest, for instance, have agreements with the University of Michigan that enable their faculty members to spend time in residence at Ann Arbor. Thus, without altering the character of the liberal arts college, these professors are able to pursue research interests.

Community colleges also have teaching as the central mission. Several years ago, the Commission on the Future of Community Colleges defined this goal precisely: "At the center of building community there is teaching. Teaching is the heartbeat of the educational enterprise and, when it is successful, energy is pumped into the community, continuously renewing and revitalizing the institution. Therefore, excellence in teaching is the means by which the vitality of the college is extended and a network of intellectual enrichment and cultural understanding is built."[10]

But here again, community college professors surely will extend their work beyond teaching and thereby enrich their work with students. Currently, about two-thirds of all community college students are enrolled in career and technical programs, so it seems reasonable to suggest that the application of knowledge would be an especially appropriate emphasis. Further, faculty on these campuses also might devote time to integrative studies, and while neither the teaching load nor facilities readily support research, this too may be found occasionally on a community college campus—especially research about teaching and learning, with special emphasis on diversity in the classroom.

Patricia Cross, of the University of California at Berkeley, has written about the "*classroom researcher*—one who is involved in the evaluation of his or her own teaching and learning, even as it takes place. Such a person should be trained to be a careful observer of the teaching process, to collect feedback on what and how well students learn, and to evaluate the effectiveness of instruction."[11] Considered in this light, teaching as a form of scholarship is particularly appropriate for community colleges.

We still have much to understand about how students learn, especially those from less advantaged backgrounds, and faculty in community colleges should be authorities on this task. George B. Vaughan, former president of Piedmont Virginia Community College, put the challenge this way: that faculty members and administrators should take "the scholarship of teaching" seriously and use a research model in evaluating and improving their teaching. If the concept of "teacher-researcher" proves to be a field of research in which community college professionals engage, then this approach to research may well emerge as the most important facet of their scholarship.[12]

The *comprehensive college or university*, perhaps more than any other, can benefit most from a redefinition of scholarship. Many of these institutions—offering a broad range of baccalaureate and master's level programs—are having a difficult time sorting out priorities. Faculty frequently come to a comprehensive college or university with one set of expectations and then are asked to fulfill others. Keith Lovin, vice president of the University of Southern Colorado, describes the problem precisely: "Often we recruit new faculty members as if we were Harvard. Seldom do we consciously try to seek out faculty members who want to be at the institutions we represent.... This, in turn, often means that there is no sense of pride for either their institution or their role in it."[13] What we urgently need are models for the comprehensive institutions, distinctive programs, and priorities that give distinctiveness to the mission and are not purposely imitative of others.

"[M]ost of the time scholarship is still equated with research and publication on our campus," write Bruce Henderson and William Kane, members of the faculty at Western Carolina University. "We have been surprised at the degree of resistance to the broader notion of scholarship. And we are at a comprehensive, not a research, university."[14] Thomas R. Lord, professor of biology at Indiana University of Pennsylvania, has written that for some, the term "scholarship" only applies to research leading to publication. "Faculty work falling outside this definition is seen as academic dabbling." This type of stereotypical thinking excludes much of the scholarly activity not only in the community college but in most of the baccalaureate and smaller institutions as well. Scholarship, instead, should be seen in a much broader context.[15]

Frank F. Wong, vice president for academic affairs at the University of Redlands, in a recent speech referred to the comprehensive university as "the ugly duckling of higher education." He went on to say: "Like interdisciplinary subjects that don't fit neatly into the established classifications of academic disciplines, they are orphans in the conventional class society of academe."[16] Wong speaks vividly of the tension he personally encountered:

> When I arrived at Redlands two and half years ago faculty members would frequently comment on the "identity problem" at the university. A significant number of faculty wanted to pursue the Pomona prototype. A smaller number wished that we were more like Stanford where professional and graduate schools set the tone and dominate the budget. Still others wanted Redlands to be like Hampshire or Evergreen, overtly unconventional and self-consciously progressive. One did not have to look far for the source of the identity problem. There was no definitive model of the comprehensive university. And somehow, the models that existed, those that faculty intuitively turn to, were a poor fit for the assemblage of activities and dynamics that are found at the comprehensive university. Because that specie of institution is so poorly defined and ill understood, those of us at such universities need to create their meaning and interpret their significance.[17]

We agree. Comprehensive colleges and universities have a unique opportunity to carve out their own distinctive missions. Rather than imitate the research university or arts and sciences model, these institutions should be viewed as campuses that blend quality and innovation. Some comprehensive colleges may choose to emphasize the scholarship of integration, encouraging interdisciplinary courses and publications, including textbooks that highlight the synthesis of knowledge. Such campuses—as *integrative* institutions—also might sponsor colloquia and all-college forums, bringing together scholars to discuss larger themes. In such a climate, faculty would be encouraged, through their scholarly work, to make connections across the disciplines, and surely they would be rewarded for such efforts.

Other comprehensive campuses might make the *application* of knowledge the centerpiece of their effort. They could, for example, give priority to programs that build bridges between teaching and practice.

Such institutions would reward faculty who establish links with institutions beyond the campus, relate the intellectual life to contemporary problems, and, in the land-grant tradition, become centers of service to the communities that surround them.

At Rollins College's Crummer Graduate School of Business, faculty are encouraged to write textbooks or articles on teaching business. "We value publication by our faculty members, but the kinds of publications we value are different," says Martin Schatz, dean of the school. He concluded: "For a large research university with doctoral programs, traditional research may be appropriate. But for a school like ours or the many others where the main work is at the undergraduate or master's level, the application of knowledge should be valued more than the development of knowledge."[18]

Some comprehensive institutions also have a special opportunity to return to their "teacher training roots," doing research on pedagogy, making the scholarship of teaching a top priority. Many of these institutions serve large groups of first-generation students. They have a rich diversity of undergraduates on campus and frequently serve older, part-time students. Building a true community of learning in the classroom and finding ways to educate diverse students and evaluate the results is a challenge that seems especially appropriate for the comprehensive college or university.

Here, then, is our conclusion. In building a truly diverse higher learning system, let's have great research centers where undergraduate instruction also will be honored. Let's have campuses where the scholarship of teaching is a central mission. Let's have colleges and universities that promote integrative studies as an exciting mission through a core curriculum, through interdisciplinary seminars, and through team teaching. And let's also have colleges and universities that give top priority to the scholarship of application, institutions that relate learning to real life in schools, in hospitals, in industry, and in business—much as the land-grant colleges worked with farmers.

What we are calling for is *diversity with dignity* in American higher education—a national network of higher learning institutions in which each college and university takes pride in its own distinctive mission and seeks to complement rather than imitate the others. While the full range of scholarship can flourish on a single campus, every college and university should find its own special niche. Why should one model dominate the system?

A NEW GENERATION OF SCHOLARS

All forms of scholarship require a broad intellectual foundation. To prepare adequately the coming generation of scholars, we must ensure the quality of both their undergraduate and graduate education. Simply stated, tomorrow's scholars must be liberally educated. They must think creatively, communicate effectively, and have the capacity and the inclination to place ideas in a larger context.

The American professoriate recently has come through a difficult time. Many of today's older faculty, following in the footsteps of their mentors, took a promising first job offer and after tenure, moved up the academic ladder, gaining recognition and prestige. For years, this system seemed to work. Then, almost overnight, new faculty faced sharply diminished opportunities. Tenure slots were restricted. Prospects for advancement narrowed. Retrenchment and lack of mobility created a highly competitive environment, spreading a sense of unease, even frustration, within the academy.

But now the pendulum may be swinging back. Career prospects are becoming brighter and the academy seems poised for a decade of renewal. Consider these statistics: In the 1984 Carnegie Foundation faculty survey, 50 percent agreed that this is a poor time for any young person to begin an academic career. In 1989, the percentage agreeing with this statement had dropped to 20 percent (table 1). We also asked in 1989: "How have

TABLE 1. THIS IS A POOR TIME FOR ANY YOUNG PERSON TO BEGIN AN ACADEMIC CAREER

	Agree	Neutral	Disagree
1984	50%	—	50%
1989	20	14	66

Source: The Carnegie Foundation for the Advancement of Teaching, *The Condition of the Professoriate: Attitudes and Trends, 1989* (Princeton, NJ, 1989), 73, 88.

job prospects for graduate students in your field changed over the past five years?" Fifty-five percent said prospects were "better"; only 13 percent felt they were getting "worse."[1] This growing sense of optimism runs across the board, covering all types of institutions (appendix table A.42).

Opportunities for new scholars are looking up; still, warning signals should be heeded. The vast army of recruits who entered academic life after the Second World War will soon retire, and for the first time in years, the nation's colleges and universities are beginning to search aggressively for a new generation of faculty. In their recent study, William G. Bowen and Julie Ann Sosa predicted a shortage of qualified professors by the year 2000, with the greatest gap in the humanities and social sciences. The authors also conclude that while demand for faculty will increase for all sectors, comprehensive universities are projected to have the greatest need.[2]

Clearly, the vitality of scholarship is threatened if the pool of recruits dwindles. As David Riesman put it, the academy must protect its seed corn and aggressive steps must be taken now to recruit into the professoriate the brightest and the best.[3] Further, concerns about tomorrow's professoriate cannot be seriously raised without focusing, with special urgency, on minority faculty, since the next generation of scholars will be challenged, as never before, by diversity in the classroom. The intolerably small pool of qualified minority applicants represents a shocking weakness, if not an indictment, of American education at all levels.

While developing a system second to none, we have failed, in this country, to cultivate an appropriately diverse faculty to staff it. Major efforts must be made to recruit minority graduate students for college faculty. As a step in the right direction, the University of Alabama at Birmingham has established a minority program of faculty development that provides summer internships for minority high school students of unusual potential. We strongly urge that every college and university join with surrounding schools to recruit black and Hispanic and Native Americans into teaching, and such programs should begin with students who are still in junior high.

In the end, the issue is not the *number* of new faculty, but the *quality* of their training. Will tomorrow's professors have an understanding of scholarship as described in this report? Will they have the capacity to place their specialized training in a larger context? If so, what kind of education will be required?

We begin with the conviction that education is a seamless web and that the quality of scholarship is being shaped, not just in graduate schools, but in the early grades. Indeed, if anything is clear from the debate about education, it is that the various levels of formal learning cannot operate in isolation and that the quality of scholarship surely begins in school, and especially in college—a time when the student's breadth of knowledge and intellectual habits will be either strengthened or diminished.

Jaroslav Pelikan, Sterling Professor of Philosophy and former dean of the Yale Graduate School, in *Scholarship and Its Survival*, calls for a major overhaul of collegiate education. He questions the traditional departmental major that today so dominates undergraduate education and concludes that the best preparation for graduate work is, in fact, a broad-based field of study. Such a focus is needed, Pelikan argues, because of "the increasingly interdisciplinary character of scholarly research."[4]

In this same spirit, we recommend in *College: The Undergraduate Experience in America* that all colleges give priority to language, defining with care a core of common learning, and we also propose what we call, "the enriched major." Such a major would run vertically, from the freshman to the senior year, interweaving general education *with* the major, and then, in the senior year, students would complete a capstone seminar. This arrangement would, we believe, put the specialty in a larger context.[5]

But it is in *graduate* education where professional attitudes and values of the professoriate are most firmly shaped; it is here that changes are most urgent if the new scholarship is to become a reality. What might be the characteristics of graduate study that would most appropriately prepare tomorrow's scholars?

We stress at the outset that most students should continue to pursue a specialized field of study and do original research. But we also are convinced that all students increasingly should be encouraged to work *across* the specialties, taking courses in other disciplines to gain a broader perspective. John Henry Cardinal Newman, in his classic work, *The Idea of a University*, argued that professional study should be located in a university precisely because such a setting would, in fact, work against narrowness of vision. It is in the university, Newman said, where students can take "a survey of all knowledge," and acquire "a special illumination and largeness of mind." Even specialized study, he insisted, should provide a liberal education, and, at its best, reflect the university's wealth of intellectual offerings.[6]

The point is that even as the categories of human knowledge have become more and more discreet, the need for interdisciplinary insight has increased. Indeed, the real danger is that graduate students will become specialists without perspective, that they will have technical competence but lack larger insights. To avoid such narrowness an integrative component should be built into every program. Specifically, we urge that all doctoral candidates be asked to put their special area of study in historical perspective and that time during graduate study also be devoted to social and ethical concerns. In such a program, the scholar should find metaphors and paradigms that give larger meaning to specialized knowledge.

In this regard, more thought should be given to the purpose and content of the dissertation. As things now stand, the dissertation is often thought of as original research, usually on an increasingly isolated topic. Consequential assertions are to be footnoted and students are discouraged from introducing ideas of their own. Creative integrative thinking often is repressed. Would it be appropriate to focus on the process of research, rather than the exclusivity of the topic? Could doctoral candidates, at the end of their dissertation, be encouraged to editorialize more about their work and place it in larger context? And, finally, could more credit be given for independent thinking?

Another way to encourage scholarly breadth is to revitalize or, as the case may be, resuscitate the dissertation "orals." As things now stand, graduate study becomes increasingly narrow, culminating in a precisely focused topic. If representatives from related fields—even specialists outside the university—were invited to read the dissertation and participate in the orals, the goal of integrating knowledge would be realized. This practice is fairly commonplace at some institutions and in some fields, but we urge that it become a reality for all so that future members of the professoriate will understand the significance of integration.

Graduate education also should be more attentive to the scholarship of application. In the current climate, graduate study is, all too often, a period of withdrawal—a time when many students are almost totally preoccupied with academic work and regulatory hurdles. In such a climate, doctoral candidates rarely are encouraged or given the opportunity to see connections between thought and action. To counter such isolation, would it be possible for graduate students to participate in a practicum experience and, in so doing, be challenged to see the larger consequence of their work and help reconnect the academy to society?

We do not suggest that graduate schools transform themselves into centers for social service or political action. The work of higher learning, at the core, is and must remain disciplined inquiry and critical thought. Still, future scholars should be asked to think about the usefulness of knowledge, to reflect on the social consequences of their work, and in so doing gain understanding of how their own study relates to the world beyond the campus. In this regard, we are impressed by "field-based" programs in medicine, business, law, and education that involve students in clinical experience and apprenticeships.

The Ford Foundation's Peter Stanley has questioned the tendency of scholars to frame their inquiry all too frequently along lines unrelated to social and civic life. "This society," Stanley said, "... suffers terribly from the separation that is opening between it and its most thoughtful members. When scholars address that need by framing their questions somewhat more broadly and writing so as to make enormously complicated issues and evidence understandable to serious lay readers, they perform a service not only to the community of scholars, but to society at large. This is an ideal that I wish graduate education in America more typically recognized and more vigorously espoused."[7]

Finally, graduate schools should give priority to teaching. As far back as 1930, G. J. Laing, dean of the graduate school at the University of Chicago, raised the essential questions: What are we doing in the way of equipping [graduate students] for their chosen work? Have the departments of the various graduate schools kept the teaching career sufficiently in mind in the organization of their program[s] of studies? Or have they arranged their courses with an eye to the production of research workers only, thinking of the teacher's duties merely as a means of livelihood, while he carries on his research?

And finally comes the question: What sort of college teachers do our [d]octors of [p]hilosophy make?[8]

The standard response is that specialized study is the best preparation for teaching. This may be true for those who teach advanced graduate or post-doctoral students. At this level, faculty and student cultures closely interact. But in teaching *undergraduates,* faculty confront circumstances in which more general knowledge and more precise pedagogical procedures are required. Helping new professors prepare for this special work is an obligation graduate schools have, all too often, overlooked. Kenneth Eble, in his book *Professors as Teachers,* registered an observation that is widely shared: "[The professor's] narrowness of vision, the disdain for education, the reluctance to function as a teacher are ills attributable in large part to graduate training. Upgrading the preparation of college teachers in graduate schools is therefore fundamentally important not only to improving teaching but to refashioning higher education."[9]

Some critics have urged a [d]octor of [a]rts degree for those interested in college teaching. It's our position that this two-track approach is not desirable. The graduate program should change, not the degree. What's needed is a requirement that teacher training be incorporated into all graduate preparation. Specifically, we urge that all graduate students participate in a seminar on teaching. Such an experience would improve classroom skills and also inform, in penetrating ways, the nature of the discipline under study. Further, by learning how to teach a phenomenon, one learns about the phenomenon itself. Ideally, the seminar on teaching would be taught collaboratively by a ranking professor in the discipline, and a colleague knowledgeable about how students learn. We also urge that the seminar be given academic credit. Anything less would suggest that teaching is just "tacked on."

Important steps are now being taken. For example, the physiology department at the State University of New York at Buffalo offers a special course on teaching biological science for its graduate students. At Indiana University, teaching assistants in the French department take a course on pedagogy that includes an overview of foreign language teaching and an examination of the theoretical bases underlying current practice. The teaching resource centers at universities such as Syracuse, the University of Washington, and the University of California, Davis, offer workshops that help academic departments prepare graduate students for teaching.

Teaching assistant programs, perhaps more than any other, are crucial in the preparation of future teachers. But the question is: How effective are they? Most "TA" arrangements are not viewed as significant academic undertakings. Graduate students are "assigned a section" but given little or no help. The primary aim is to give senior faculty relief and help graduate students meet financial obligations. The needs of those being taught are often not seriously considered. The situation is exacerbated when the most accomplished graduate students are given *research* assistantships—and rewarded by *not* having to teach. One TA put it this way: "Teaching is considered secondary at best, with the implication being that those who aspire to teach or who enjoy it are not good scholars or intellects. The department gives double messages about teaching. It does not want to short-change the undergrads, but it is suspicious of those of us who care deeply about teaching."[10]

Yet, the situation is improving. Universities all across the country are focusing on the role of TAs. National conferences on the subject are being held, and we urge that every TA participate in a seminar on teaching. We also urge that English proficiency be a prerequisite for such an assignment.

The University of California at San Diego was one of the first institutions in the country to require new TAs to complete a training program. The heart of San Diego's fifteen-year-old effort is a two-part seminar that covers such issues as teaching goals and course design. TAs discuss the problems they're facing after just a few weeks on the job, including how to stimulate class participation and field difficult questions. In addition, more seasoned TAs become "teaching consultants" to new recruits. The veteran TAs are also videotaped so they can evaluate and improve their own teaching.

One final point. Graduate students, in preparing to teach, also might be asked to work with mentors—veteran faculty who have distinguished themselves by the quality of their instruction. This approach is being used widely to prepare young people to teach in elementary and secondary schools. In higher education, a close and continuing relationship between a graduate teaching assistant and a gifted teacher can be an enriching experience for both. The observations, consultations, and discussions about the nature of teaching surely would help foster critical inquiry into good practice.

In 1987, in a presentation to the Council of Colleges of Arts and Sciences, Daniel Fallon, dean of the college of liberal arts at Texas A&M University, described, in a wonderfully revealing way, his own graduate school experience that captures the essence of the inspired preparation we envision. Here was a doctoral candidate in experimental psychology being advised by his mentor to think about good teaching, and above all, to reflect on the values that sustain life itself. Fallon writes:

> More than twenty-five years ago I was finishing my Ph.D. work at the University of Virginia in experimental psychology. I was extremely fortunate to have encountered as a mentor Professor Frank W. Finger, who led a seminar designed for doctoral students in their final year. In it, Frank prepared us for academic life by having us discuss professional

> codes of ethics, write sample grant proposals, and structure our early careers, and, above all, by preparing us to teach. He had us develop lectures for various kinds of undergraduate courses, which were then criticized and redone, and we prepared different sorts of examinations and discussed principles of grading. During the spring semester he told us that there was to be a public university-wide lecture that evening by a professor from Yale who was regarded as an outstanding teacher. He urged us to attend, if we had time, in order to observe an example of good teaching.
>
> That evening was one of the high points of my life. I went alone. The lecturer was J. Vincent Scully and his topic was the history of western art and architecture. The lights were dimmed so that he could illustrate his narrative with slides depicting great works of art from antiquity to modern times. I was transported. His lecture was like flowing liquid, with one valuable idea cascading rapidly upon another, building cumulative force throughout the hour. At the end he summarized the lesson of the human spirit, as revealed through its art, in an engaging seven-word message, recurrent throughout the ages. This enduring instruction also captures the essence of my concern with the value of process. So I feel free to charge you with it today. What humanity has been telling us, Scully said, is "Love, act, or as a species perish!"[11]

Surely, much of what goes on in graduate education today is worth preserving. Graduate schools must continue to be a place where students experience the satisfaction that comes from being on the cutting edge of a field, and the dissertation, or a comparable project, should continue to be the centerpiece—the intellectual culmination of the graduate experience. However, it is our conviction that if scholarship is to be redefined, graduate study must be broadened, encompassing not only research, but integration, application, and teaching, too. It is this vision that will [en]sure, we believe, a new generation of scholars, one that is more intellectually vibrant and more responsive to society's shifting needs.

SCHOLARSHIP AND COMMUNITY

As we move toward a new century, profound changes stir the nation and the world. The contours of a new order—and the dimensions of new challenges—loom large on the horizon. It is a moment for boldness in higher education and many are now asking: How can the role of the scholar be defined in ways that not only affirm the past but also reflect the present and adequately anticipate the future?

We have set forth in this report a view of scholarship that is, we believe, more appropriate to the changing conditions. We strongly affirm the importance of research—what we have called the scholarship of discovery. Without the vigorous pursuit of free and open inquiry this country simply will not have the intellectual capacity it needs to resolve the huge, almost intractable social, economic, and ecological problems, both national and global. Nor will the academy itself remain vital if it fails to enlarge its own store of human knowledge. But to define the work of the professoriate narrowly—chiefly in terms of the research model—is to deny many powerful realities. It is our central premise, therefore, that other forms of scholarship—teaching, integration, and application—must be fully acknowledged and placed on a more equal footing with discovery.

There is growing evidence that professors want, and need, better ways for the full range of their aspirations and commitments to be acknowledged. Faculty are expressing serious reservations about the enterprise to which they have committed their professional lives. This deeply rooted professional concern reflects, we believe, recognition that teaching is crucial, that integrative studies are increasingly consequential, and that, in addition to research, the work of the academy must relate to the world beyond the campus.

Higher education leaders are acknowledging that diversity brings with it important new obligations. We have, on campuses today, students of many backgrounds. Colleges and universities are being called upon to respond to a large and increasingly varied group of students, many of whom have special talents, as well as special needs. In response, greater attention to students, to teaching, to the curriculum, are being demanded. There is a recognition that faculty obligations must extend beyond the classroom and that both the academic and civic dimensions of collegiate life must be carefully molded to serve the new constituencies.

Beyond the campus, colleges and universities are being asked to account for what they do and to rethink their relevance in today's world. Throughout the years great social advances have been initiated by scholars in America's universities; still, linkages between the campus and contemporary problems must be strengthened. Derek Bok, president of Harvard, warns of the dangers of detachment when he writes: "Armed with the security of tenure and the time to study the world with care, professors would appear to have a unique opportunity to act as society's scouts to signal impending problems long before they are visible to others. Yet rarely have members of the academy succeeded in discovering the emerging issues and bringing them vividly to the attention of the public."[1]

President Bok further observes that "what Rachel Carson did for risks to the environment, Ralph Nader for consumer protection, Michael Harrington for problems of poverty, Betty Friedan for women's rights, they did as independent critics, not as members of a faculty. Even the seminal work on the plight of blacks in America was written by a Swedish social scientist, not by a member of an American university. After a major social problem has been recognized," Bok concludes, "universities will usually continue to respond weakly unless outside support is available and the subjects involved command prestige in academic circles. These limitations have hampered efforts to address many of the most critical challenges to the nation."[2]

Clearly, higher education and the rest of society have never been more interdependent than they are today, and embedded in Bok's pointed observations is a call for campuses to be more energetically engaged in the pressing issues of our time. Our world has undergone immense transformations. It has become a more crowded, less stable place. The human community is increasingly interdependent, and higher education must focus with special urgency on questions that affect profoundly the destiny of all: How can the quality of the environment be sustained? Should the use of nuclear energy be expanded or cut back? Can an adequate supply of food and water be [en]sured? How can our limited natural resources be allocated to meet our vast social needs? What new structures of world order can be devised to cope with the challenges of the post–cold war era?

Even the baffling questions of just when human life begins and ends must be seriously examined against the backdrop of transcendent moral and ethical implications. Now is the time, we conclude, to build bridges across the disciplines and connect the campus to the larger world. Society itself has a great stake in how scholarship is defined.

The nation's schools, its health care delivery system, and its banking system, for instance, all cry out for the application of knowledge that faculty can provide. New discoveries, rooted in research, can today, as in the past, produce cures for dreaded diseases and improve the quality of life. Other problems that relate, for example, to the environment, to ethical and social issues, to crime and poverty also require more carefully crafted study and, indeed, solutions that rely not only on new knowledge but on integration, too. And surely the scholarship of teaching will be necessary to produce an informed citizenry capable of the critical thinking that is so needed in America today.

The conclusion is clear. We need scholars who not only skillfully explore the frontiers of knowledge but also integrate ideas, connect thought to action, and inspire students. The very complexity of modem life requires more, not less, information; more, not less, participation. If the nation's colleges and universities cannot help students see beyond themselves and better understand the interdependent nature of our world, each new generation's capacity to live responsibly will be dangerously diminished.

This point, properly understood, warns against making too great a distinction between careerism and the liberal arts, between self-benefit and service. The aim of education is not only to prepare students for productive careers but also to enable them to live lives of dignity and purpose; not only to generate new knowledge but [also] to channel that knowledge to humane ends; not merely to study government but to help shape a citizenry that can promote the public good. Thus, higher education's vision must be widened if the nation is to be rescued from problems that threaten to diminish permanently the quality of life.

The challenge is to strengthen research, integration, application, and teaching. Such a broad, energetic view of scholarship will not emerge, however, without strong leadership at the top. Indeed, the president, more than any other person, can give shape and direction to a college and create a climate in which priorities of the professoriate can be appropriately considered. Does the president, for example, push the campus primarily toward national recognition or serving local needs? Does the president truly believe that undergraduates are not only to be aggressively recruited but also to be given full support once they enroll? And is it agreed that faculty who spend time in service will be appropriately recognized and rewarded? How, in fact, is institutional status and recognition administratively defined? What the president has to say about these matters surely will be consequential in determining the priorities of the campus.

The point is this: The modern college or university president has leverage on the formulation of policy because of the respect and visibility of the office. He or she often controls discretionary funds that can work as "pump primers" for creative projects. The president has access to legislative committees, foundations, corporate offices, and other sources of support that can encourage innovation. Further, there is a growing tendency for tenure and promotion policies to be centrally controlled. Mainly, presidents have, or should have, the power of persuasion. They can speak with a powerful voice, and we urge that presidents use the office to define scholarly priorities wisely and create campus forums where such proposals can be thoughtfully debated. Appeals to a larger vision are limited only by the ingenuity and commitments of the leader.

But, when all is said and done, faculty themselves must assume primary responsibility for giving scholarship a richer, more vital meaning. Professors are, or should be, keepers of the academic gates.

They define the curriculum, set standards for graduation, and determine criteria by which faculty performance will be measured—and rewarded. Today, difficult choices about institutional mission and professional priorities must be made. Only as faculty help shape their purposes and engage actively in policy formulation will a broader view of scholarship be authentically embraced.

Much of this important work is carried on through committees. But faculty senates also must be actively involved, and, further, new all-college forums are needed, places to discuss academic priorities that cut across departmental interests. We are concerned, however, that administrative centralization may be causing faculty governance to decline at the very moment higher learning faces the challenge of renewal. To counter such a trend, we urge that topics such as "scholarship and its uses" become a matter of campuswide discussion—with faculty committees and the faculty senate serving as the focal points for such discourse.

In shaping priorities of the professoriate, professional associations also have a crucial role to play. The Modem Language Association, for example, has begun to organize institutes on teaching—forums for intellectual exchange that encourage an integrative view of scholarship. Recently, the American Mathematical Association asked faculty across the country to investigate why so many students fail college calculus courses. The inquiry caused teachers to review the curriculum and consider more carefully their own pedagogical procedures. We are especially encouraged by the leadership of the American Council of Learned Societies, [which] has placed increased emphasis on teaching and has linked university scholars in liberal arts fields to teachers in the nation's schools. These significant efforts help give legitimacy to scholarship in all its forms.

Finally, accrediting bodies can contribute to scholarship as redefined. Today, regional accrediting associations, at least in theory, measure each college and university on the basis of its own distinctive mission. For this, they should be applauded. In reality, however, there is still a tendency for visiting teams to judge colleges and universities quite conservatively, using traditional norms that inhibit innovations and restrict the full range of scholarly endeavors. Especially disturbing is the way professional accrediting associations dictate detailed regulations and, in the process, violate the integrity of the campus, pushing institutions toward conformity.

If the potential of American higher education is to be fully recognized, standards must be flexible and creative. Campuses should be encouraged to pursue their own distinctive missions, and innovation should be rewarded, not restricted. Would it be possible, for example, for visiting teams to ask graduate schools to report on how doctoral students are being prepared for teaching? Could a college be asked to demonstrate how its institutional mission relates to criteria for faculty tenure or promotion? Would it be possible for accreditation teams to ask campuses how procedures for faculty assessment have been developed—and whether they encourage the full range of scholarship?

One last point. This report has focused largely on faculty members, as *individuals.* But professors, to be fully effective, cannot work continuously in isolation. It is toward a *shared* vision of intellectual and social possibilities—a community of scholars—that the four dimensions of academic endeavor should lead. In the end, scholarship at its best should bring faculty together.

A campuswide, collaborative effort around teaching would be mutually enriching. A similar case can be made for cooperative research, as investigators talk increasingly about "networks of knowledge," even as individual creativity is recognized and affirmed. Integrative work, by its very definition, cuts across the disciplines. And in the application of knowledge, the complex social and economic and political problems of our time increasingly require a *team* approach.

The team approach, which seems so necessary for individuals, applies to institutions, too. Looking to the future, why not imagine a vital national network of colleges and universities with great diversity and one in which the full range of human talent is celebrated and recorded? In such a system, the discovery of knowledge, the integration of knowledge, the application of knowledge, and great teaching would be fully honored, powerfully reinforcing one another. If the vision of scholarship can be so enlarged on *every* campus, it seems reasonable to expect that across the entire country a true community of scholarship will emerge, one that is not only more collaborative, but more creative, too.

American higher education has never been static. For more than 350 years, it has shaped its programs in response to the changing social context. And as we look at today's world, with its disturbingly complicated problems, higher learning, we conclude, must, once again, adapt. It would be foolhardy not to reaffirm the accomplishments of the past. Yet, even the best of our institutions must continuously evolve.

And to sustain the vitality of higher education in *our* time, a new vision of scholarship is required, one dedicated not only to the renewal of the academy but, ultimately, to the renewal of society itself.

APPENDIX A

NATIONAL SURVEY OF FACULTY (1989)

TABLE A.1. IN MY DEPARTMENT IT IS DIFFICULT FOR A PERSON TO ACHIEVE TENURE IF HE OR SHE DOES NOT PUBLISH

	Strongly Agree	Agree with Reservations	Neutral	Disagree with Reservations	Strongly Disagree
All respondents	**42%**	**12%**	**9%**	**10%**	**27%**
Four-year	60	17	4	11	8
Two-year	4	2	18	9	67
Research	83	12	1	3	2
Doctorate-granting	71	18	2	6	3
Comprehensive	43	23	6	16	12
Liberal arts	24	16	9	26	25
Two-year	4	2	18	9	67
Biological sciences	52	12	5	5	27
Business	42	10	9	8	31
Education	46	15	5	12	23
Engineering	63	18	7	7	4
Fine arts	21	15	14	18	32
Health sciences	37	13	10	16	25
Humanities	43	12	7	12	27
Physical sciences	46	11	9	7	27
Social sciences	52	10	5	7	26
Other	28	11	16	11	35
Male	45	13	9	9	25
Female	35	10	8	13	34
Less than 40 years old	53	13	7	8	19
40 years or more	39	12	9	10	29

TABLE A.2. MULTIDISCIPLINARY WORK IS SOFT AND SHOULD NOT BE CONSIDERED SCHOLARSHIP

	Strongly Agree	Agree with Reservations	Neutral	Disagree with Reservations	Strongly Disagree
All respondents	**2%**	**6%**	**17%**	**26%**	**49%**
Four-year	2	5	12	27	54
Two-year	2	7	27	24	39
Research	2	5	9	27	57
Doctorate-granting	2	4	13	25	55
Comprehensive	3	5	14	27	
Liberal arts	2	6	16	28	49
Two-year	2	7	27	24	39
Biological sciences	2	7	17	22	53
Business	2	3	27	31	37
Education	2	5	18	22	53
Engineering	2	7	19	33	39
Fine arts	4	4	22	23	47
Health sciences	0	8	11	33	48
Humanities	2	6	13	25	53
Physical sciences	1	7	18	32	42
Social sciences	2	6	11	21	60
Other	3	5	20	27	45
Male	2	7	17	28	46
Female	2	2	18	22	56
Less than 40 years old	2	4	14	27	54
40 years or more	2	6	18	26	48

TABLE A.3. IN MY DISCIPLINE, MOST FACULTY AGREE ON THE STANDARDS OF GOOD SCHOLARSHIP

	Strongly Agree	Agree with Reservations	Neutral	Disagree with Reservations	Strongly Disagree
All respondents	**17%**	**27%**	**13%**	**22%**	**22%**
Four-year	20	28	12	21	19
Two-year	11	25	15	23	27
Research	25	31	11	18	15
Doctorate-granting	21	30	12	20	16
Comprehensive	17	25	13	24	21

TABLE A.3. Continued

	Strongly Agree	Agree with Reservations	Neutral	Disagree with Reservations	Strongly Disagree
Liberal arts	10	21	10	22	38
Two-year	11	25	15	23	27
Biological sciences	19	33	13	19	16
Business	12	25	21	22	20
Education	19	26	9	23	23
Engineering	14	29	20	18	20
Fine arts	21	23	14	22	20
Health sciences	12	35	6	15	32
Humanities	21	30	9	22	19
Physical sciences	10	21	15	27	27
Social sciences	22	26	12	17	22
Other	14	25	14	24	23
Male	17	27	14	22	19
Female	17	24	10	20	29
Less than 40 years old	23	26	14	19	17
40 years or more	16	27	13	22	23

TABLE A.4. FACULTY IN MY DEPARTMENT HAVE FUNDAMENTAL DIFFERENCES ABOUT THE NATURE OF THE DISCIPLINE

	Strongly Agree	Agree with Reservations	Neutral	Disagree with Reservations	Strongly Disagree
All respondents	**17%**	**27%**	**13%**	**22%**	**22%**
Four-year	20	28	12	21	19
Two-year	11	25	15	23	27
Research	25	31	11	18	15
Doctorate-granting	21	30	12	20	16
Comprehensive	17	25	13	24	21
Liberal arts	10	21	10	22	38
Two-year	11	25	15	23	27
Biological sciences	19	33	13	19	16
Business	12	25	21	22	20
Education	19	26	9	23	23
Engineering	14	29	20	18	20

(*continued*)

TABLE A.4. Continued

	Strongly Agree	Agree with Reservations	Neutral	Disagree with Reservations	Strongly Disagree
Fine arts	21	23	14	22	20
Health sciences	12	35	6	15	32
Humanities	21	30	9	22	19
Physical sciences	10	21	15	27	27
Social sciences	22	26	12	17	22
Other	14	25	14	24	23
Male	17	27	14	22	19
Female	17	24	10	20	29
Less than 40 years old	23	26	14	19	17
40 years or more	16	27	13	22	23

TABLE A.5. HOW IMPORTANT IS THE NUMBER OF PUBLICATIONS FOR GRANTING TENURE IN YOUR DEPARTMENT?

	Very Important	Fairly Important	Fairly Unimportant	Very Unimportant	No Opinion
All respondents	**28%**	**29%**	**14%**	**22%**	**7%**
Four-year	41	39	11	7	2
Two-year	2	8	19	54	17
Research	56	39	4	1	1
Doctorate-granting	55	36	6	2	1
Comprehensive	30	42	15	10	3
Liberal arts	8	32	31	23	6
Two-year	2	8	19	54	17
Biological sciences	38	27	13	19	3
Business	37	18	11	26	7
Education	34	29	13	20	5
Engineering	43	40	10	5	3
Fine arts	13	36	17	25	10
Health sciences	25	28	13	20	13
Humanities	26	34	14	21	5
Physical sciences	24	33	16	21	7
Social sciences	36	30	11	22	1
Other	20	21	15	30	15
Male	29	31	13	20	6
Female	25	24	15	28	9
Less than 40 years old	38	29	11	16	6
40 years or more	26	29	14	24	7

TABLE A.6. HOW IMPORTANT ARE STUDENT EVALUATIONS OF COURSES TAUGHT FOR GRANTING TENURE IN YOUR DEPARTMENT?

	Very Important	Fairly Important	Fairly Unimportant	Very Unimportant	No Opinion
All respondents	**26%**	**41%**	**19%**	**10%**	**4%**
Four-year	25	43	21	10	2
Two-year	29	37	15	10	9
Research	10	41	30	16	2
Doctorate-granting	19	42	26	11	1
Comprehensive	37	43	13	4	2
Liberal arts	45	45	6	1	3
Two-year	29	37	15	10	9
Biological sciences	19	44	20	15	2
Business	27	39	15	11	8
Education	36	40	13	7	4
Engineering	17	38	31	10	4
Fine arts	29	44	12	7	7
Health sciences	29	42	13	7	9
Humanities	24	39	24	10	3
Physical sciences	23	46	17	10	3
Social sciences	27	39	20	12	1
Other	28	38	20	8	6
Male	24	42	20	9	5
Female	33	37	16	10	4
Less than 40 years old	26	35	22	12	5
40 years or more	26	42	18	9	4

TABLE A.7. HOW IMPORTANT ARE OBSERVATIONS OF TEACHING BY COLLEAGUES AND/OR ADMINISTRATORS FOR GRANTING TENURE IN YOUR DEPARTMENT?

	Very Important	Fairly Important	Fairly Unimportant	Very Unimportant	No Opinion
All respondents	**23%**	**31%**	**19%**	**21%**	**6%**
Four-year	13	30	23	29	5
Two-year	43	34	10	4	9
Research	4	23	29	39	5
Doctorate-granting	6	25	27	36	7

(continued)

TABLE A.7. Continued

	Very Important	Fairly Important	Fairly Unimportant	Very Unimportant	No Opinion
Comprehensive	20	37	17	20	5
Liberal arts	29	40	14	11	6
Two-year	43	34	10	4	9
Biological sciences	18	31	21	25	5
Business	22	29	16	25	8
Education	21	31	20	22	6
Engineering	7	30	29	29	5
Fine arts	26	38	13	15	7
Health sciences	23	34	18	14	11
Humanities	23	35	19	19	4
Physical sciences	28	31	17	18	5
Social sciences	19	26	21	28	6
Other	28	31	16	16	9
Male	19	32	20	22	6
Female	32	30	15	16	7
Less than 40 years old	22	29	19	21	9
40 years or more	23	32	18	21	6

TABLE A.8. HOW IMPORTANT ARE RECOMMENDATIONS FROM OUTSIDE SCHOLARS FOR GRANTING TENURE IN YOUR DEPARTMENT?

	Very Important	Fairly Important	Fairly Unimportant	Very Unimportant	No Opinion
All respondents	**21%**	**24%**	**21%**	**24%**	**11%**
Four-year	29	29	19	16	7
Two-year	3	16	24	38	19
Research	53	30	8	6	3
Doctorate-granting	29	36	16	13	6
Comprehensive	9	25	30	26	10
Liberal arts	16	26	25	23	11
Two-year	3	16	24	38	19
Biological sciences	28	23	16	27	7
Business	10	20	22	31	16
Education	17	28	20	26	9
Engineering	31	26	21	14	8
Fine arts	19	31	20	19	11

TABLE A.8. Continued

	Very Important	Fairly Important	Fairly Unimportant	Very Unimportant	No Opinion
Health sciences	17	23	20	15	24
Humanities	21	26	23	23	6
Physical sciences	30	22	16	23	9
Social sciences	23	25	22	23	8
Other	14	22	23	26	15
Male	22	24	21	23	10
Female	17	24	21	25	13
Less than 40 years old	24	26	18	20	12
40 years or more	20	24	21	24	10

TABLE A.9. HOW IMPORTANT ARE RESEARCH GRANTS RECEIVED BY THE SCHOLAR FOR GRANTING TENURE IN YOUR DEPARTMENT?

	Very Important	Fairly Important	Fairly Unimportant	Very Unimportant	No Opinion
All respondents	**20%**	**30%**	**19%**	**23%**	**8%**
Four-year	28	38	19	11	4
Two-year	3	14	18	47	18
Research	40	36	16	6	2
Doctorate-granting	35	40	16	7	2
Comprehensive	19	43	20	13	5
Liberal arts	9	29	31	23	7
Two-year	3	14	18	47	18
Biological sciences	37	32	8	20	4
Business	9	27	21	31	12
Education	21	40	12	21	6
Engineering	49	28	17	4	2
Fine arts	14	31	20	21	14
Health sciences	32	24	17	11	16
Humanities	10	34	25	26	6
Physical sciences	28	30	15	19	8
Social sciences	17	34	23	23	3
Other	18	23	18	28	14
Male	21	31	19	22	7
Female	19	29	17	25	10
Less than 40 years old	26	30	17	19	9
40 years or more	19	30	19	24	8

TABLE A.10. HOW IMPORTANT ARE THE REPUTATIONS OF THE PRESSES OR JOURNALS PUBLISHING THE BOOKS OR ARTICLES FOR GRANTING TENURE IN YOUR DEPARTMENT?

	Very Important	Fairly Important	Fairly Unimportant	Very Unimportant	No Opinion
All respondents	**19%**	**27%**	**19%**	**26%**	**9%**
Four-year	28	38	19	12	3
Two-year	2	5	18	55	19
Research	40	43	12	3	1
Doctorate-granting	32	41	17	8	2
Comprehensive	18	36	23	18	5
Liberal arts	7	26	29	28	9
Two-year	2	5	18	55	19
Biological sciences	22	32	17	25	4
Business	25	21	15	30	10
Education	22	28	20	24	6
Engineering	28	35	27	6	4
Fine arts	13	24	20	32	10
Health sciences	16	29	15	24	16
Humanities	19	30	20	25	5
Physical sciences	18	31	17	25	8
Social sciences	20	34	17	26	3
Other	14	18	19	31	18
Male	20	29	19	24	8
Female	16	24	18	31	11
Less than 40 years old	23	32	16	21	8
40 years or more	18	27	19	27	9

TABLE A.11. HOW IMPORTANT ARE RECOMMENDATIONS FROM OTHER FACULTY WITHIN THE INSTITUTION FOR GRANTING TENURE IN YOUR DEPARTMENT?

	Very Important	Fairly Important	Fairly Unimportant	Very Unimportant	No Opinion
All respondents	**17%**	**38%**	**24%**	**14%**	**7%**
Four-year	18	40	24	13	4
Two-year	15	35	22	16	11
Research	15	40	27	14	4
Doctorate-granting	13	40	26	16	5

TABLE A.11. Continued

	Very Important	Fairly Important	Fairly Unimportant	Very Unimportant	No Opinion
Comprehensive	19	39	24	13	5
Liberal arts	38	41	13	4	4
Two-year	15	35	22	16	11
Biological sciences	20	43	16	17	5
Business	13	42	20	17	8
Education	18	41	21	13	7
Engineering	16	45	28	7	5
Fine arts	18	40	20	14	8
Health sciences	19	46	15	7	13
Humanities	15	41	27	13	4
Physical sciences	18	40	22	14	7
Social sciences	14	32	32	17	5
Other	21	32	24	15	9
Male	15	39	26	14	6
Female	22	37	17	15	9
Less than 40 years old	21	42	16	11	10
40 years or more	16	37	25	15	6

TABLE A.12. HOW IMPORTANT IS SERVICE WITHIN THE UNIVERSITY COMMUNITY FOR GRANTING TENURE IN YOUR DEPARTMENT?

	Very Important	Fairly Important	Fairly Unimportant	Very Unimportant	No Opinion
All respondents	**14%**	**37%**	**28%**	**15%**	**6%**
Four-year	11	37	33	16	3
Two-year	19	39	19	14	10
Research	3	23	46	25	4
Doctorate-granting	6	37	37	18	2
Comprehensive	17	47	23	10	3
Liberal arts	27	51	14	4	4
Two-year	19	39	19	14	10
Biological sciences	15	32	35	14	4
Business	14	35	28	17	8
Education	15	41	25	15	4
Engineering	5	29	46	18	3
Fine arts	21	42	21	9	7

(continued)

TABLE A.12. Continued

	Very Important	Fairly Important	Fairly Unimportant	Very Unimportant	No Opinion
Health sciences	16	42	20	10	11
Humanities	14	40	27	15	3
Physical sciences	11	36	29	19	6
Social sciences	11	38	31	17	3
Other	14	36	26	15	8
Male	10	38	31	15	5
Female	22	35	21	15	6
Less than 40 years old	12	35	29	17	8
40 years or more	14	38	27	15	5

TABLE A.13. HOW IMPORTANT ARE RECOMMENDATIONS FROM CURRENT OR FORMER STUDENTS FOR GRANTING TENURE IN YOUR DEPARTMENT?

	Very Important	Fairly Important	Fairly Unimportant	Very Unimportant	No Opinion
All respondents	**11%**	**31%**	**25%**	**26%**	**7%**
Four-year	9	30	27	28	5
Two-year	15	33	21	21	11
Research	3	21	33	39	5
Doctorate-granting	6	25	32	32	5
Comprehensive	13	38	23	21	5
Liberal arts	30	42	13	9	6
Two-year	15	33	21	21	11
Biological sciences	9	32	27	28	4
Business	6	23	30	29	13
Education	13	34	21	26	5
Engineering	5	24	35	30	6
Fine arts	13	38	23	19	7
Health sciences	16	31	20	21	11
Humanities	12	31	26	26	5
Physical sciences	9	35	26	23	6
Social sciences	11	28	24	33	4
Other	13	31	23	23	10
Male	9	31	27	26	7
Female	17	30	20	25	7
Less than 40 years old	11	27	26	28	8
40 years or more	11	32	25	26	7

TABLE A.14. HOW IMPORTANT IS SERVICE WITHIN THE SCHOLAR'S DISCIPLINE FOR GRANTING TENURE IN YOUR DEPARTMENT?

	Very Important	Fairly Important	Fairly Unimportant	Very Unimportant	No Opinion
All respondents	**9%**	**42%**	**28%**	**15%**	**7%**
Four-year	10	48	30	9	4
Two-year	7	29	23	26	15
Research	6	44	35	11	3
Doctorate-granting	8	51	29	9	3
Comprehensive	13	51	26	7	4
Liberal arts	11	43	29	11	6
Two-year	7	29	23	26	15
Biological sciences	7	48	27	14	3
Business	9	38	29	15	10
Education	16	47	20	12	6
Engineering	7	39	38	12	5
Fine arts	19	42	18	15	6
Health sciences	8	50	12	13	17
Humanities	7	42	32	14	4
Physical sciences	7	41	31	14	8
Social sciences	5	43	31	16	5
Other	8	36	29	17	11
Male	7	43	29	14	6
Female	13	38	24	16	9
Less than 40 years old	10	34	35	12	10
40 years or more	8	43	27	15	7

TABLE A.15. HOW IMPORTANT ARE SYLLABI FOR COURSES TAUGHT FOR GRANTING TENURE IN YOUR DEPARTMENT?

	Very Important	Fairly Important	Fairly Unimportant	Very Unimportant	No Opinion
All respondents	**9%**	**22%**	**26%**	**34%**	**8%**
Four-year	5	19	29	41	6
Two-year	18	28	20	22	12
Research	1	11	29	54	5
Doctorate-granting	2	13	30	48	6
Comprehensive	9	25	29	30	7
Liberal arts	14	38	25	17	6

(continued)

TABLE A.15. Continued

	Very Important	Fairly Important	Fairly Unimportant	Very Unimportant	No Opinion
Two-year	18	28	20	22	12
Biological sciences	7	21	30	38	5
Business	6	19	27	36	12
Education	12	20	24	36	7
Engineering	2	17	34	40	6
Fine arts	11	21	29	28	11
Health sciences	16	20	21	28	16
Humanities	8	24	29	33	5
Physical sciences	8	19	27	38	8
Social sciences	10	23	22	41	4
Other	11	26	22	28	12
Male	7	21	27	36	8
Female	14	24	23	30	9
Less than 40 years old	7	20	26	38	10
40 years or more	10	23	26	34	8

TABLE A.16. HOW IMPORTANT ARE LECTURES OR PAPERS DELIVERED AT PROFESSIONAL MEETINGS OR AT OTHER COLLEGES AND UNIVERSITIES FOR GRANTING TENURE IN YOUR DEPARTMENT?

	Very Important	Fairly Important	Fairly Unimportant	Very Unimportant	No Opinion
All respondents	**7%**	**41%**	**27%**	**18%**	**7%**
Four-year	9	51	28	10	3
Two-year	3	20	24	37	16
Research	8	45	33	12	2
Doctorate-granting	8	53	29	8	2
Comprehensive	12	56	22	8	3
Liberal arts	7	46	30	10	6
Two-year	3	20	24	37	16
Biological sciences	7	44	26	19	4
Business	9	29	30	24	8
Education	9	53	15	19	4
Engineering	8	41	39	9	3
Fine arts	8	42	21	20	9

TABLE A.16. Continued

	Very Important	Fairly Important	Fairly Unimportant	Very Unimportant	No Opinion
Health sciences	14	41	20	14	11
Humanities	6	46	27	18	4
Physical sciences	6	42	28	15	8
Social sciences	6	38	32	20	4
Other	7	34	26	20	13
Male	7	41	28	18	7
Female	9	40	24	20	7
Less than 40 years old	7	41	27	17	7
40 years or more	7	40	26	19	7

TABLE A.17. HOW IMPORTANT ARE PUBLISHED REVIEWS OF THE SCHOLAR'S BOOKS FOR GRANTING TENURE IN YOUR DEPARTMENT?

	Very Important	Fairly Important	Fairly Unimportant	Very Unimportant	No Opinion
All respondents	**5%**	**16%**	**29%**	**36%**	**14%**
Four-year	6	22	34	26	11
Two-year	1	4	18	56	21
Research	8	26	35	22	9
Doctorate-granting	7	24	36	23	9
Comprehensive	5	20	34	29	13
Liberal arts	3	16	32	37	12
Two-year	1	4	18	56	21
Biological sciences	3	9	27	44	16
Business	4	7	28	42	19
Education	5	21	28	36	10
Engineering	7	15	42	19	17
Fine arts	8	21	21	30	19
Health sciences	3	13	31	31	22
Humanities	7	22	29	33	8
Physical sciences	2	13	32	37	17
Social sciences	4	21	30	40	6
Other	3	13	26	38	20
Male	5	17	30	35	13
Female	4	14	27	39	16
Less than 40 years old	5	13	30	33	19
40 years or more	4	17	29	37	13

TABLE A.18. HOW IMPORTANT IS ACADEMIC ADVISEMENT FOR GRANTING TENURE IN YOUR DEPARTMENT?

	Very Important	Fairly Important	Fairly Unimportant	Very Unimportant	No Opinion
All respondents	**5%**	**20%**	**30%**	**36%**	**9%**
Four-year	5	17	31	40	7
Two-year	6	27	27	27	13
Research	1	8	31	52	8
Doctorate-granting	2	11	31	49	7
Comprehensive	6	24	33	30	7
Liberal arts	15	34	27	17	7
Two-year	6	27	27	27	13
Biological sciences	3	22	29	38	8
Business	3	22	23	39	13
Education	7	23	32	30	8
Engineering	4	11	38	38	9
Fine arts	9	24	27	33	7
Health sciences	10	21	28	25	16
Humanities	3	17	34	38	8
Physical sciences	2	22	34	32	10
Social sciences	6	17	30	41	7
Other	6	22	25	35	11
Male	4	19	32	37	9
Female	8	22	26	33	10
Less than 40 years old	4	17	31	36	12
40 years or more	5	21	30	36	9

TABLE A.19. APPROXIMATELY HOW MANY ARTICLES HAVE YOU EVER PUBLISHED IN ACADEMIC OR PROFESSIONAL JOURNALS?

	None	One To Five	Six to Ten	Eleven or More
All respondents	**26%**	**33%**	**13%**	**28%**
Four-year	13	30	17	40
Two-year	52	38	6	4
Research	4	16	16	63
Doctorate-granting	9	27	21	42
Comprehensive	19	41	17	24
Liberal arts	32	42	12	15
Two-year	52	38	6	4
Biological sciences	8	27	15	51

TABLE A.19. Continued

	None	One To Five	Six to Ten	Eleven or More
Business	33	35	8	24
Education	22	34	16	29
Engineering	9	25	13	53
Fine arts	45	37	8	10
Health sciences	29	42	13	16
Humanities	23	35	18	24
Physical sciences	20	30	9	41
Social sciences	19	33	16	32
Other	42	31	11	16
Male	22	30	13	35
Female	36	39	13	13
Less than 40 years old	27	39	16	19
40 years or more	26	31	13	30

TABLE A.20. APPROXIMATELY HOW MANY BOOKS OR MONOGRAPHS HAVE YOU EVER PUBLISHED OR EDITED, ALONE OR IN COLLABORATION?

	None	One To Five	Six to Ten	Eleven or More
All respondents	**56%**	**38%**	**4%**	**2%**
Four-year	49	43	5	3
Two-year	69	28	2	1
Research	38	51	7	4
Doctorate-granting	47	46	5	2
Comprehensive	57	38	3	2
Liberal arts	67	30	2	1
Two-year	69	28	2	1
Biological sciences	60	40	1	0
Business	56	38	4	2
Education	55	37	5	3
Engineering	62	32	4	1
Fine arts	69	28	1	2
Health sciences	73	26	1	0
Humanities	42	49	6	3
Physical sciences	64	31	4	1
Social sciences	49	43	5	3
Other	58	37	3	2

(continued)

TABLE A.20. Continued

	None	One To Five	Six to Ten	Eleven or More
Male	52	41	5	3
Female	65	33	2	1
Less than 40 years old	71	28	1	1
40 years or more	53	40	4	2

TABLE A.21. ARE YOU CURRENTLY ENGAGED IN ANY SCHOLARLY WORK THAT YOU EXPECT TO LEAD TO A PUBLICATION, AN EXHIBIT, OR A MUSICAL RECITAL?

	Yes	No
All respondents	**66%**	**34%**
Four-year	84	16
Two-year	32	68
Research	95	5
Doctorate-granting	89	11
Comprehensive	75	25
Liberal arts	68	32
Two-year	32	68
Biological sciences	78	22
Business	54	46
Education	60	40
Engineering	80	20
Fine arts	81	19
Health sciences	64	36
Humanities	71	29
Physical sciences	68	32
Social sciences	71	29
Other	50	50
Male	69	31
Female	60	40
Less than 40 years old	79	21
40 years or more	63	37

TABLE A.22. DURING THE PAST TWELVE MONTHS, DID YOU ATTEND ANY NATIONAL PROFESSIONAL MEETINGS?

	Yes	No
All respondents	**68%**	**32%**
Four-year	76	24
Two-year	48	52
Research	86	14
Doctorate-granting	78	22
Comprehensive	69	31
Liberal arts	65	35
Two-year	48	52
Biological sciences	75	25
Business	61	39
Education	80	20
Engineering	79	21
Fine arts	60	40
Health sciences	69	31
Humanities	66	34
Physical sciences	65	35
Social sciences	65	35
Other	67	33
Male	68	32
Female	66	34
Less than 40 years old	73	27
40 years or more	67	33

TABLE A.23. TEACHING EFFECTIVENESS SHOULD BE THE PRIMARY CRITERION FOR PROMOTION OF FACULTY

	Strongly Agree	Agree with Reservations	Neutral	Disagree with Reservations	Strongly Disagree
All respondents	**32%**	**30%**	**7%**	**18%**	**13%**
Four-year	20	27	9	25	19
Two-year	56	36	3	3	1
Research	6	15	9	36	34
Doctorate-granting	14	27	11	30	18
Comprehensive	31	37	8	17	7
Liberal arts	38	38	6	12	6

(continued)

TABLE A.23. Continued

	Strongly Agree	Agree with Reservations	Neutral	Disagree with Reservations	Strongly Disagree
Two-year	56	36	3	3	1
Biological sciences	21	30	7	20	22
Business	37	30	5	16	12
Education	41	29	8	14	9
Engineering	28	17	9	23	22
Fine arts	37	36	9	12	5
Health sciences	36	35	6	14	9
Humanities	26	36	6	20	13
Physical sciences	23	28	7	21	20
Social sciences	25	25	9	24	17
Other	46	31	5	12	6
Male	29	28	7	19	15
Female	39	35	5	14	7
Less than 40 years old	28	25	8	24	15
40 years or more	33	31	7	17	12

TABLE A.24. AT MY INSTITUTION PUBLICATIONS USED FOR TENURE AND PROMOTION ARE JUST COUNTED, NOT QUALITATIVELY MEASURED

	Strongly Agree	Agree with Reservations	Neutral	Disagree with Reservations	Strongly Disagree
All respondents	**14%**	**24%**	**25%**	**18%**	**19%**
Four-year	17	30	13	25	15
Two-year	8	11	50	4	27
Research	15	27	9	30	19
Doctorate-granting	19	34	10	26	12
Comprehensive	20	34	14	22	10
Liberal arts	12	21	27	20	21
Two-year	8	11	50	4	27
Biological sciences	20	27	22	15	15
Business	18	27	22	16	17
Education	14	31	20	20	15
Engineering	16	34	14	23	14
Fine arts	12	22	31	17	18

TABLE A.24. Continued

	Strongly Agree	Agree with Reservations	Neutral	Disagree with Reservations	Strongly Disagree
Health sciences	12	24	23	19	22
Humanities	16	21	21	20	22
Physical sciences	10	22	30	21	17
Social sciences	14	24	19	22	21
Other	12	20	37	12	20
Male	14	24	25	20	18
Female	16	22	25	15	22
Less than 40 years old	15	26	27	19	13
40 years or more	14	23	24	18	20

TABLE A.25. AT MY INSTITUTION WE NEED BETTER WAYS, BESIDES PUBLICATIONS, TO EVALUATE THE SCHOLARLY PERFORMANCE OF THE FACULTY

	Strongly Agree	Agree with Reservations	Neutral	Disagree with Reservations	Strongly Disagree
All respondents	**39%**	**29%**	**19%**	**9%**	**5%**
Four-year	41	33	12	10	4
Two-year	35	20	33	5	7
Research	35	34	12	14	4
Doctorate-granting	44	33	10	10	4
Comprehensive	48	32	11	7	3
Liberal arts	37	32	16	10	5
Two-year	35	20	33	5	7
Biological sciences	32	30	21	12	5
Business	44	24	21	7	4
Education	47	33	10	7	2
Engineering	40	41	12	7	1
Fine arts	51	26	16	4	3
Health sciences	52	25	15	5	2
Humanities	35	29	18	12	6
Physical sciences	28	33	23	11	5
Social sciences	35	27	19	12	6
Other	43	23	24	5	5

(*continued*)

TABLE A.25. Continued

	Strongly Agree	Agree with Reservations	Neutral	Disagree with Reservations	Strongly Disagree
Male	38	30	19	10	4
Female	43	25	20	6	5
Less than 40 years old	39	28	18	11	4
40 years or more	39	29	19	8	5

TABLE A.26. DO YOUR INTERESTS LIE PRIMARILY IN RESEARCH OR IN TEACHING?

	Research	Leaning to Research	Leaning to Teaching	Teaching
All respondents	**6%**	**24%**	**26%**	**44%**
Four-year	9	33	32	26
Two-year	1	6	15	78
Research	18	48	24	9
Doctorate-granting	8	37	35	20
Comprehensive	3	20	38	39
Liberal arts	2	15	34	49
Two-year	1	6	15	78
Biological sciences	15	30	22	33
Business	7	17	25	51
Education	2	15	30	53
Engineering	7	43	23	27
Fine arts	3	23	39	36
Health sciences	2	23	26	48
Humanities	6	25	32	37
Physical sciences	7	29	20	44
Social sciences	10	29	24	37
Other	3	14	23	59
Male	7	26	26	41
Female	4	18	28	50
Less than 40 years old	11	33	25	31
40 years or more	5	22	27	47

TABLE A.27. DURING THE PAST TWELVE MONTHS, DID YOU (OR YOUR PROJECT) RECEIVE RESEARCH SUPPORT FROM INSTITUTIONAL OR DEPARTMENTAL FUNDS?

	Yes	No
All respondents	**42%**	**58%**
Four-year	51	49
Two-year	23	77
Research	59	41
Doctorate-granting	55	45
Comprehensive	43	57
Liberal arts	45	55
Two-year	23	77
Biological sciences	59	41
Business	37	63
Education	33	67
Engineering	48	52
Fine arts	37	63
Health sciences	50	50
Humanities	43	57
Physical sciences	41	59
Social sciences	47	53
Other	36	64
Male	42	58
Female	41	59
Less than 40 years old	56	44
40 years or more	39	61

TABLE A.28. DURING THE PAST TWELVE MONTHS, DID YOU (OR YOUR PROJECT) RECEIVE RESEARCH SUPPORT FROM FEDERAL AGENCIES?

	Yes	No
All respondents	**18%**	**82%**
Four-year	24	76
Two-year	5	95
Research	43	57
Doctorate-granting	19	81
Comprehensive	10	90
Liberal arts	11	89

(*continued*)

TABLE A.28. Continued

	Yes	No
Two-year	5	95
Biological sciences	41	59
Business	7	93
Education	11	89
Engineering	47	53
Fine arts	3	97
Health sciences	18	82
Humanities	10	90
Physical sciences	35	65
Social sciences	16	84
Other	11	89
Male	19	81
Female	14	86
Less than 40 years old	24	76
40 years or more	16	84

TABLE A.29. DURING THE PAST TWO OR THREE YEARS, FINANCIAL SUPPORT FOR WORK IN MY DISCIPLINE HAS BECOME HARDER TO OBTAIN

	Strongly Agree	Agree with Reservations	Neutral	Disagree with Reservations	Strongly Disagree
All respondents	**30%**	**24%**	**31%**	**12%**	**3%**
Four-year	32	26	27	12	3
Two-year	26	21	40	11	2
Research	38	25	21	13	3
Doctorate-granting	33	27	25	12	3
Comprehensive	27	26	31	12	4
Liberal arts	28	25	35	10	3
Two-year	26	21	40	11	2
Biological sciences	41	22	25	10	2
Business	16	19	42	17	6
Education	39	25	24	10	2
Engineering	29	23	34	12	2
Fine arts	45	19	24	9	3
Health sciences	32	32	16	17	3
Humanities	26	23	37	11	3

TABLE A.29. Continued

	Strongly Agree	Agree with Reservations	Neutral	Disagree with Reservations	Strongly Disagree
Physical sciences	27	28	34	9	3
Social sciences	32	23	32	10	2
Other	24	25	32	15	3
Male	29	24	32	12	3
Female	33	23	29	12	3
Less than 40 years old	32	23	32	11	2
40 years or more	29	24	32	12	3

TABLE A.30. MY JOB IS THE SOURCE OF CONSIDERABLE PERSONAL STRAIN

	Strongly Agree	Agree with Reservations	Neutral	Disagree with Reservations	Strongly Disagree
All respondents	**12%**	**32%**	**11%**	**27%**	**18%**
Four-year	14	32	11	27	15
Two-year	8	30	10	29	23
Research	15	32	12	24	16
Doctorate-granting	12	34	12	26	15
Comprehensive	14	31	11	29	15
Liberal arts	12	35	11	26	16
Two-year	8	30	10	29	23
Biological sciences	13	34	9	20	25
Business	10	23	13	31	22
Education	12	31	10	28	20
Engineering	16	33	18	20	12
Fine arts	19	36	9	24	11
Health sciences	12	43	11	17	18
Humanities	12	32	10	30	16
Physical sciences	6	29	10	32	23
Social sciences	11	28	11	32	18
Other	13	34	11	25	16
Male	11	30	12	29	19
Female	16	36	8	24	17
Less than 40 years old	16	37	13	23	11
40 years or more	11	30	10	28	20

TABLE A.31. I HARDLY EVER GET TIME TO GIVE A PIECE OF WORK THE ATTENTION IT DESERVES

	Strongly Agree	Agree with Reservations	Neutral	Disagree with Reservations	Strongly Disagree
All respondents	**12%**	**32%**	**13%**	**31%**	**12%**
Four-year	13	34	13	28	11
Two-year	9	27	13	37	14
Research	13	33	12	30	13
Doctorate-granting	14	32	15	29	11
Comprehensive	14	37	13	26	11
Liberal arts	13	34	11	31	11
Two-year	9	27	13	37	14
Biological sciences	14	32	11	30	12
Business	11	27	15	30	18
Education	7	36	12	32	13
Engineering	22	29	15	24	9
Fine arts	17	32	13	23	14
Health sciences	13	25	9	34	18
Humanities	11	34	10	34	11
Physical sciences	83	1	15	34	12
Social sciences	9	31	17	31	13
Other	13	33	12	32	10
Male	10	32	14	31	13
Female	15	32	9	32	12
Less than 40 years old	16	37	13	27	7
40 years or more	11	31	13	32	14

TABLE A.32. THE PRESSURE TO PUBLISH REDUCES THE QUALITY OF TEACHING AT MY UNIVERSITY

	Strongly Agree	Agree with Reservations	Neutral	Disagree with Reservations	Strongly Disagree
All respondents	**16%**	**19%**	**19%**	**19%**	**27%**
Four-year	20	26	12	24	19
Two-year	8	6	33	9	44
Research	24	29	10	23	15
Doctorate-granting	23	31	11	22	14
Comprehensive	18	23	13	25	21

TABLE A.32. Continued

	Strongly Agree	Agree with Reservations	Neutral	Disagree with Reservations	Strongly Disagree
Liberal arts	8	14	16	28	34
Two-year	8	6	33	9·	44
Biological sciences	20	20	13	15	32
Business	16	19	18	16	31
Education	18	25	15	20	21
Engineering	24	29	13	19	15
Fine arts	13	20	28	17	22
Health sciences	20	16	18	27	20
Humanities	14	17	14	23	32
Physical sciences	11	20	23	21	26
Social sciences	17	19	14	22	29
Other	15	16	28	12	28
Male	15	20	19	20	26
Female	17	17	19	17	31
Less than 40 years old	19	24	19	18	20
40 years or more	15	18	19	19	29

TABLE A.33. EXCITING DEVELOPMENTS ARE NOW TAKING PLACE IN MY DISCIPLINE

	Strongly Agree	Agree with Reservations	Neutral	Disagree with Reservations	Strongly Disagree
All respondents	**47%**	**30%**	**12%**	**8%**	**4%**
Four-year	46	32	12	7	3
Two-year	48	27	11	9	4
Research	47	30	12	7	3
Doctorate-granting	46	32	13	6	3
Comprehensive	45	32	11	8	4
Liberal arts	43	33	14	7	3
Two-year	48	27	11	9	4
Biological sciences	80	14	3	3	0
Business	35	37	20	4	4
Education	41	37	11	7	4
Engineering	55	28	11	4	2

(continued)

TABLE A.33. Continued

	Strongly Agree	Agree with Reservations	Neutral	Disagree with Reservations	Strongly Disagree
Fine arts	40	27	15	13	5
Health sciences	50	34	8	5	3
Humanities	32	37	14	14	4
Physical sciences	59	28	9	3	1
Social sciences	38	29	16	13	5
Other	54	27	8	6	6
Male	46	30	12	8	3
Female	48	30	10	7	5
Less than 40 years old	52	30	10	6	3
40 years or more	46	30	12	8	4

TABLE A.34. I TEND TO SUBORDINATE ALL ASPECTS OF MY LIFE TO MY WORK

	Strongly Agree	Agree with Reservations	Neutral	Disagree with Reservations	Strongly Disagree
All respondents	**11%**	**30%**	**9%**	**30%**	**20%**
Four-year	12	33	10	29	17
Two-year	9	24	8	34	25
Research	13	33	9	27	17
Doctorate-granting	10	32	9	30	19
Comprehensive	12	32	10	29	17
Liberal arts	13	33	10	29	15
Two-year	9	24	8	34	25
Biological sciences	12	32	10	25	21
Business	8	33	8	25	26
Education	9	30	11	31	20
Engineering	20	33	11	21	15
Fine arts	18	35	9	24	14
Health sciences	12	18	10	36	23
Humanities	11	31	9	31	18
Physical sciences	6	29	11	32	21
Social sciences	8	27	9	33	24
Other	13	29	6	34	19

TABLE A.34. Continued

	Strongly Agree	Agree with Reservations	Neutral	Disagree with Reservations	Strongly Disagree
Male	10	29	10	30	21
Female	13	31	7	31	18
Less than 40 years old	14	33	8	30	15
40 years or more	10	29	9	30	21

TABLE A.35. I AM MORE ENTHUSIASTIC ABOUT MY WORK NOW THAN I WAS WHEN I BEGAN MY ACADEMIC CAREER

	Strongly Agree	Agree with Reservations	Neutral	Disagree with Reservations	Strongly Disagree
All respondents	**16%**	**28%**	**22%**	**21%**	**12%**
Four-year	16	27	24	21	12
Two-year	18	29	18	22	13
Research	15	26	26	21	12
Doctorate-granting	15	24	25	23	14
Comprehensive	16	29	22	20	13
Liberal arts	18	29	23	21	9
Two-year	18	29	18	22	13
Biological sciences	17	21	26	25	12
Business	18	26	24	21	11
Education	15	27	21	22	14
Engineering	15	25	28	18	14
Fine arts	23	23	22	19	13
Health sciences	18	28	18	23	13
Humanities	17	28	20	21	15
Physical sciences	14	27	27	22	10
Social sciences	15	29	22	20	14
Other	16	34	18	22	10
Male	15	27	24	22	12
Female	19	29	18	21	13
Less than 40 years old	15	31	24	21	8
40 years or more	17	27	22	21	13

TABLE A.36. IF 1 HAD IT TO DO OVER AGAIN, I WOULD NOT BECOME A COLLEGE TEACHER

	Strongly Agree	Agree with Reservations	Neutral	Disagree with Reservations	Strongly Disagree
All respondents	**6%**	**8%**	**8%**	**24%**	**53%**
Four-year	7	9	9	25	51
Two-year	6	7	7	21	58
Research	6	7	11	25	51
Doctorate-granting	8	8	10	26	48
Comprehensive.	7	10	7	25	51
Liberal arts	6	8	8	23	55
Two-year	6	7	7	21	58
Biological sciences	7	8	8	19	57
Business	5	8	10	23	54
Education	8	7	9	23	54
Engineering	8	5	11	21	54
Fine arts	7	10	9	23	51
Health sciences	5	9	10	30	46
Humanities	7	9	6	20	57
Physical sciences	6	9	9	25	51
Social sciences	7	8	8	23	54
Other	5	8	8	28	51
Male	6	9	9	24	52
Female	7	7	7	24	56
Less than 40 years old	6	8	9	30	47
40 years or more	6	8	8	22	55

TABLE A.37. I FEEL TRAPPED IN A PROFESSION WITH LIMITED OPPORTUNITY FOR ADVANCEMENT

	Strongly Agree	Agree with Reservations	Neutral	Disagree with Reservations	Strongly Disagree
All respondents	**6%**	**13%**	**10%**	**21%**	**50%**
Four-year	6	12	11	21	50
Two-year	7	15	9	20	50
Research	5	9	10	19	56
Doctorate-granting	7	13	10	20	50
Comprehensive	7	15	11	23	44

TABLE A.37. Continued

	Strongly Agree	Agree with Reservations	Neutral	Disagree with Reservations	Strongly Disagree
Liberal arts	6	12	10	23	50
Two-year	7	15	9	20	50
Biological sciences	5	14	14	19	48
Business	4	10	8	23	55
Education	4	14	10	24	49
Engineering	6	10	13	16	56
Fine arts	12	16	11	18	43
Health sciences	10	14	10	20	45
Humanities	6	13	8	19	54
Physical sciences	5	10	9	23	53
Social sciences	6	13	8	24	49
Other	7	15	11	18	48
Male	6	13	11	21	50
Female	8	13	8	20	50
Less than 40 years old	5	18	12	22	43
40 years or more	7	12	10	20	52

TABLE A.38. PLEASE INDICATE THE DEGREE TO WHICH YOUR ACADEMIC DISCIPLINE IS IMPORTANT TO YOU

	Very Important	Fairly Important	Fairly Unimportant	Not at All Important
All respondents	**77%**	**21%**	**2%**	**0%**
Four-year	76	22	2	0
Two-year	81	17	2	0
Research	77	21	2	0
Doctorate-granting	75	23	2	0
Comprehensive	75	23	2	0
Liberal arts	77	21	2	0
Two-year	81	17	2	0
Biological sciences	82	17	0	0
Business	70	26	3	1
Education	80	19	1	0
Engineering	75	23	2	0
Fine arts	91	9	0	0

(*continued*)

TABLE A.38. Continued

	Very Important	Fairly Important	Fairly Unimportant	Not at All Important
Health sciences	85	14	1	0
Humanities	78	20	2	0
Physical sciences	76	23	1	0
Social sciences	70	25	5	0
Other	76	22	2	0
Male	75	23	2	0
Female	83	16	1	0
Less than 40 years old	78	19	3	0
40 years or more	77	21	2	0

TABLE A.39. PLEASE INDICATE THE DEGREE TO WHICH YOUR DEPARTMENT IS IMPORTANT TO YOU

	Very Important	Fairly Important	Fairly Unimportant	Not at All Important
All respondents	**53%**	**37%**	**8%**	**1%**
Four-year	51	38	9	2
Two-year	58	34	6	1
Research	48	39	11	2
Doctorate-granting	48	41	8	3
Comprehensive	52	37	9	1
Liberal arts	59	35	5	1
Two-year	58	34	6	1
Biological sciences	55	34	8	3
Business	48	44	8	1
Education	54	37	8	1
Engineering	52	42	6	0
Fine arts	58	37	4	1
Health sciences	63	33	4	0
Humanities	50	36	12	2
Physical sciences	51	38	9	1
Social sciences	48	37	12	3
Other	60	34	5	0
Male	52	38	9	1
Female	57	35	7	1
Less than 40 years old	46	43	10	1
40 years or more	55	36	8	1

TABLE A.40. PLEASE INDICATE THE DEGREE TO WHICH YOUR COLLEGE OR UNIVERSITY IS IMPORTANT TO YOU

	Very Important	Fairly Important	Fairly Unimportant	Not at All Important
All respondents	**40%**	**45%**	**12%**	**2%**
Four-year	35	48	14	3
Two-year	51	40	8	1
Research	30	50	17	4
Doctorate-granting	34	47	16	3
Comprehensive	36	48	12	3
Liberal arts	53	38	8	1
Two-year	51	40	8	1
Biological sciences	43	40	13	4
Business	39	47	12	2
Education	50	42	6	2
Engineering	41	43	16	1
Fine arts	40	47	10	3
Health sciences	36	53	11	0
Humanities	38	45	13	4
Physical sciences	37	49	13	1
Social sciences	35	45	16	3
Other	46	43	10	2
Male	39	45	13	2
Female	43	45	10	2
Less than 40 years old	28	53	16	3
40 years or more	43	44	11	2

TABLE A.41. THIS IS A POOR TIME FOR ANY YOUNG PERSON TO BEGIN AN ACADEMIC CAREER

	Strongly Agree	Agree with Reservations	Neutral	Disagree with Reservations	Strongly Disagree
All respondents	**6%**	**14%**	**14%**	**35%**	**31%**
Four-year	7	14	15	37	27
Two-year	4	14	11	32	39
Research	7	15	16	38	24
Doctorate-granting	7	15	14	37	26

(continued)

TABLE A.41. Continued

	Strongly Agree	Agree with Reservations	Neutral	Disagree with Reservations	Strongly Disagree
Comprehensive	7	13	16	36	28
Liberal arts	4	12	12	40	31
Two-year	4	14	11	32	39
Biological sciences	7	12	12	34	35
Business	5	13	16	29	37
Education	4	14	13	35	34
Engineering	11	17	15	32	25
Fine arts	9	13	19	30	29
Health sciences	2	10	13	26	49
Humanities	5	18	13	39	25
Physical sciences	6	12	15	36	32
Social sciences	5	14	15	37	30
Other	7	12	11	40	30
Male	6	14	15	36	29
Female	6	13	12	34	35
Less than 40 years old	8	12	16	41	23
40 years or more	5	14	13	34	33

TABLE A.42. HOW HAVE JOB PROSPECTS FOR GRADUATE STUDENTS IN YOUR FIELD CHANGED OVER THE PAST FIVE YEARS?

	Much Better	Somewhat Better	About the Same	Somewhat Worse	Much Worse
All respondents	**25%**	**30%**	**32%**	**10%**	**3%**
Four-year	25	33	31	9	2
Two-year	24	25	34	12	5
Research	23	34	30	10	3
Doctorate-granting	25	34	30	9	2
Comprehensive	28	31	31	9	1
Liberal arts	22	35	32	8	3
Two-year	24	25	34	12	5
Biological sciences	18	35	32	10	5
Business	26	33	36	4	0
Education	28	21	33	16	3
Engineering	28	30	38	4	0

TABLE A.42. Continued

	Much Better	Somewhat Better	About the Same	Somewhat Worse	Much Worse
Fine arts	9	14	51	20	6
Health sciences	68	15	15	3	0
Humanities	19	40	28	10	4
Physical sciences	30	34	27	8	1
Social sciences	18	36	32	11	3
Other	29	26	31	10	3
Male	23	31	33	10	2
Female	31	28	28	9	4
Less than 40 years old	25	31	29	12	4
40 years or more	25	30	32	10	3

APPENDIX B

TECHNICAL NOTES

The Carnegie Foundation data presented in this report represent the responses of faculty from across the nation at all types of institutions. The 1989 National Survey of Faculty was conducted for the Carnegie Foundation for the Advancement of Teaching by the Wirthlin Group of McLean, Virginia. Questionnaires were mailed to nearly [ten thousand] faculty members; usable returns numbered 5,450, a 54.5 percent completion rate.

A two-stage, stratified, random sample design was used. In the first stage, colleges and universities—both four-year and two-year—were selected; in the second, faculty were designated. For each of the nine Carnegie classification types, approximately thirty-four institutions were selected for a total of 306 colleges and universities. Within each classification category a school was selected with a likelihood proportionate to the size of its faculty compared to the others within that type.

For selecting faculty within the designated institutions, an *n*th name selection process was used. The 9,996 faculty in the sample were equally divided among Carnegie classification types.

For conducting analyses, faculty responses are weighted by Carnegie classification categories. The weight used for each type is proportionate to its relative size within the total for all types. Size is defined as the total number of faculty [members].

The 1989 and 1984 data presented in this report represent full-time campus faculty members. The 1989 figures refer to all respondents. Some figures in the tables may not add up to 100 percent due to rounding of decimals. In several of the tables "strongly agree" and "agree with reservations" have been combined to represent "agree"; "strongly disagree" and "disagree with reservations" have been combined to represent "disagree."

A more detailed description of the results from the 1989 National Survey of Faculty can be found in *The Condition of the Professoriate: Attitudes and Trends, 1989*, available from the Princeton University Press, 3175 Princeton Pike, Lawrenceville, New Jersey 08648 (telephone 609-896-1344). For additional information on data presented in this report, contact the Carnegie Foundation for the Advancement of Teaching, 5 Ivy Lane, Princeton, New Jersey 08540.

APPENDIX C

CARNEGIE CLASSIFICATIONS

The 1987 Carnegie classification includes all colleges and universities in the United States listed in the 1985–1986 Higher Education General Information Survey of Institutional Characteristics. It groups institutions into categories on the basis of the level of degree offered, ranging from pre-baccalaureate to the doctorate, and the comprehensiveness of their missions. The categories are as follows:

Research Universities I: These institutions offer a full range of baccalaureate programs, are committed to graduate education through the doctorate degree, and give high priority to research. They receive annually at least $33.5 million in federal support and award at least fifty PhD degrees each year.

Research Universities II: These institutions offer a full range of baccalaureate programs, are committed to graduate education through the doctorate degree, and give high priority to research. They receive annually at least $12.5 million in federal support and award at least fifty PhD degrees each year.

Doctorate-granting Universities I: In addition to offering a full range of baccalaureate programs, the mission of these institutions includes a commitment to graduate education through the doctorate degree. They award at least forty PhD degrees annually in five or more academic disciplines.

Doctorate-granting Universities II: In addition to offering a full range of baccalaureate programs, the mission of these institutions includes a commitment to graduate education through the doctorate degree. They award annually twenty or more PhD degrees in at least one discipline or ten or more PhD degrees in three or more disciplines.

Comprehensive Universities and Colleges I: These institutions offer baccalaureate programs and, with few exceptions, graduate education through the master's degree. More than half of their baccalaureate degrees are awarded in two or more occupational or professional disciplines such as engineering or business administration. All of the institutions in this group enroll at least 2,500 students.

Comprehensive Universities and Colleges II: These institutions award more than half of their baccalaureate degrees in two or more occupational or professional disciplines, such as engineering or business administration, and many also offer graduate education through the master's degree. All of the institutions in this group enroll between 1,500 and 2,500 students.

Liberal Arts Colleges I: These highly selective institutions are primarily undergraduate colleges that award more than half of their baccalaureate degrees in art and science fields.

Liberal Arts Colleges II: These institutions are primarily undergraduate colleges that are less selective and award more than half of their degrees in liberal arts fields. This category also includes a group of colleges that award less than half of their degrees in liberal arts fields but, with fewer than 1,500 students, are too small to be considered comprehensive.

Two-Year Community, Junior, and Technical Colleges: These institutions offer certificate or degree programs through the associate of arts level and, with few exceptions, offer no baccalaureate degrees.

AFTERWORD: ADVANCING THE CONVERSATION AROUND *SCHOLARSHIP RECONSIDERED*

Cynthia A. Wells

Highher education is at a crossroads, one both familiar to and distinct from the social and educational context surrounding the publication of *Scholarship Reconsidered.* As the chapters in this book remind us, Boyer faced a set of challenges comparable to what we face today. Similar to a quarter century ago, higher education is encountering consequential and dynamic change—declining public confidence, pervasive questions about the faculty member roles, and concerns about quality and relevance, to name only a few. Today's climate also adds to these formidable challenges by posing new questions focused on increasing access in a context of greater accountability, the unbundling of the faculty member role while enhancing student learning, and declining resources even as demands escalate. *Scholarship Reconsidered* raised our collective consciousness as to the nature and purpose of the academic vocation then and have the capacity to do so now.

Boyer's aim was to bring a "broader, more capacious meaning" to scholarship, as Mary Taylor Huber's foreword astutely points out. As higher education scholars and leaders consider the influence of *Scholarship Reconsidered,* it is crucial that we ask, "a broader, more capacious meaning" for what purpose? "For what purpose" is a deeply *Boyer-esque* question;[1] thus, it is apropos that we ground our exploration of the continuing relevance of *Scholarship Reconsidered* on Boyer's essential intentions. He aimed to bring "legitimacy to the full scope of academic work" by reorienting the priorities of the professoriate.[2] Toward that end, Boyer reminded his audience of the original indicators of excellence for the scholarly profession—to think well and to continuously learn but also to "step back from one's investigation, to find connections, to build bridges between theory and practice, and to communicate one's knowledge effectively to students."[3] As this book illustrates, tremendous progress has been made in advancing a wider vision of scholarship. Still, much work remains in order to bring validity to the wide-ranging span of academic work. If we stop there, however, we have done ourselves and Boyer's vision a grave disservice.

The point is not to legitimize an expanded view of scholarship as an end in and of itself but rather to honor the full range of activities of the academic vocation in order to effectively educate students and serve society. Drew Moser and Todd C. Ream's chapter reminds us that the focus of Boyer's work was the student. A key milestone in ascertaining the impact of *Scholarship Reconsidered* is thus how its scholarly framework and systems of accountability affect students. Even the emphasis on the student experience was a means to a greater end for Boyer because the ultimate indicator of quality in higher education was the well-being of society. This alignment of educational programs with the societal needs is what Boyer meant when he called for coherence in higher education.[4] This call for coherence is certainly relevant today as we engage fundamental concerns regarding alignment between faculty member values and the priorities for student learning in our contemporary educational and social context.

Toward bettering society, Boyer believed deeply in a model of American higher education that supported a wide range of institutional types. In *Scholarship Reconsidered,* he aimed to enrich, not diminish, that diversity. As John M. Braxton's chapter clarifies, Boyer emphasized that the type of scholarship stressed should align with institutional identity and mission. The scholarly role must attend to all four functions, but different institutional contexts accentuate particular domains. For example, a liberal arts college may privilege the scholarly functions of teaching and integration whereas a research university would stress the scholarship of discovery. *Scholarship Reconsidered* has contributed richly to renewal in a manner that honors institutional variety.

Boyer's ideas, as expressed in *Scholarship Reconsidered,* resonate in a multitude of very specific innovations. As Andrea L. Beach illustrates, the notion of a scholarship of teaching has profoundly affected faculty member development, both in its maturation as a field and its practices, even becoming a "signature" program offered by faculty development professionals. Her chapter, as well as the chapter by Ann E. Austin and Melissa McDaniels, emphasize the relationship between *Scholarship Reconsidered* and faculty learning communities. Professional associations and related journals concerning the particular dimensions of scholarship have been created. We have *Scholarship Reconsidered* to thank for a wealth of such specific improvement efforts in higher education.

The ultimate gift of *Scholarship Reconsidered* is its provision of a new vocabulary—a resounding theme across each chapter in this book. Austin and McDaniels describe it best by saying that Boyer's work provided a "conceptual anchor" that, in turn, produced a generative and expansive vocabulary for a national dialogue on scholarship. Boyer was a master in reconsidering conceptual foundations and reorienting our questions. *Scholarship Reconsidered* reflects this gift by reminding us of the roots of the academic profession and forcing us to think anew about how those roots come to fruition in new contexts. The gifts in Boyer's work are manifest in how his concepts ground and reorient our thinking.

Moreover, his attentiveness to the broad context of higher education in the United States necessitated breadth and openness. As was true with Boyer's hopes for campus community[5] and general education,[6] he provided a broad framework that would fit multiple contexts. *Scholarship Reconsidered* raised our collective consciousness regarding the point of scholarship, providing a vision for reengaging untapped dimensions of the scholarly role and illustrating ways these ideas may come to pass in various institutional contexts.

The flipside of this strength is a lack of specificity when it comes to implementing these concepts in specific institutional contexts. Thus, one cannot simply read *Scholarship Reconsidered* if one is to be faithful in its application today. Much has been accomplished in applying the ideals of *Scholarship Reconsidered* to tenure and promotion policies.[7] As Huber's foreword documents, the follow-up Carnegie report, *Scholarship Assessed,* identified standards that provide a "shared arc for scholarship," including well-defined goals, sufficient preparation, suitable methods, significant outcomes, effective presentation, and reflective critique. Furthermore, Austin and McDaniel's chapter emphasizes that all forms of scholarship benefit from documentation and public assessment. We have unequivocally advanced our shared understanding of the varied demands of scholarship in the twenty-five years since the initial publication of *Scholarship Reconsidered.*

Despite such advances, Rubin's critique that *Scholarship Reconsidered* would lead to a "scholarship of confusion" has in some ways rung true.[8]

We must turn to the rich collection of follow-up work that better differentiates good teaching from the scholarship of teaching as well as distinguishes valuable and noble community service from the scholarship of engagement. It is time to clarify that reconsidering the nature of the professoriate and the dimensions of scholarship within that profession does not mean that "scholarship" is a catch-all for everything. As O'Meara's chapter documents this all-too-common misperception, the point is not a lower threshold for quality scholarship. In fact, we do Boyer's vision a disservice if we dilute the academic vocation rather than imbue it with greater precision.

Being mindful of Boyer's intent for the interconnectedness of scholarly functions helps us realize their rigor. The scholarship of discovery, integration, application and engagement, and teaching were conceptualized as "four separate, yet overlapping, functions" rather than divergent realms of scholarship. The scholarship of teaching involves genuine discovery as to what constitutes good teaching. The scholarship of engagement involves deliberate integration of intellectual rigor with application to real-world problems. At its core, *Scholarship Reconsidered* makes scholarship more rather than less rigorous even as it extends the mantle of the intellectual endeavor in more expansive directions.

Scholarship Reconsidered provided sketches of the four scholarly functions of discovery, integration, application and engagement, and teaching, and the past twenty-five years have given birth to fuller definitions of these functions and to professional societies that advocate their particular relevance. This is all to the good as long as it does not pull us further apart. If the four functions of the professoriate become separate and distinct guilds in the contemporary academy, bounded by professional identities and associations, these scholarly functions are misappropriated and actually contribute to the overspecialization and fragmentation in the academy that Boyer intended to mitigate in *Scholarship Reconsidered* and other works.[9] If we are to be true to Boyer's vision, scholarship must be an interconnected set of practices rather than a new set of professional identities.

Beyond reclaiming and clarifying the essential conceptual commitments that undergird *Scholarship Reconsidered,* there is specific work yet to be accomplished. Given Boyer's attentiveness to connection, it is ironic that the notion of scholarship as integration has been the least examined dimension in the past twenty-five years. Further exploration of the scholarship of integration is a worthy endeavor. In addition, much work remains in order to establish indicators that more effectively assess scholarly productivity in ways that clearly hold faculty members accountable to excellence. As Braxton's chapter documents, we have much work to do to expand the traditional templates for assessing faculty member scholarship beyond traditional publications, a limitation that greatly misrepresents the productivity of faculty members in comprehensive colleges, liberal arts colleges, and community colleges.

Finally, O'Meara notes that implementing more expansive definitions of scholarship in tenure and promotion have helped campuses become more distinct in their mission and ethos. As a result, further exploration of the benefits of *Scholarship Reconsidered* for differentiation of institutional types and combatting "mission creep" in higher education is warranted. Clearly, aspects of *Scholarship Reconsidered* remain untapped.

As the essays in Part One have illustrated, the last twenty-five years have led to extraordinary advances in our understanding of scholarship, to developing strong communities of practice, and to disseminating research that exemplifies the importance of various functions of scholarship. As higher education finds itself at new crossroads, the questions raised in *Scholarship Reconsidered* become more rather than less relevant. The ideas advanced in *Scholarship Reconsidered* have permeated higher education and substantively affected our thinking and renewal efforts. These concepts now give rise to new queries: What are the implications of the scholarly functions of the professoriate in an era of unbundling? How can the various dimensions of scholarship contribute to enhancing access and student learning? How can this more capacious meaning of scholarship serve to reclaim public confidence and advance higher education's contribution to the well-being of society?

Attending to these and other questions lies at the heart of the mission of the Ernest L. Boyer Center at Messiah College. Our primary concern is to create space for considering how Boyer's convictions and priorities may be applied to current educational challenges. In *Scholarship Reconsidered,* Boyer started a conversation. As evident in this critical book, many voices have contributed to the dialogue. It is our task as higher education scholars and leaders to further the conversation. The Boyer Center, both in its vast archival collection of Boyer's works and in its programs, serves as a rich resource for considering Boyer's vision for higher education in the present and future. At the same time, the center offers a clearinghouse for new questions. Indeed, the leading query we receive as a center is that of how the functions of scholarship—discovery, integration, application and engagement, and teaching—are applied in tenure and promotion policies; this lends credence to the need for further dialogue and exploration. This critical introduction illustrates how deeply this work resonates with our deepest needs from scholarship in higher education, and I am certain there is an audience ripe for this conversation.

DISCUSSION GUIDE

Foreword

1. Mary Taylor Huber suggested higher education was at a crossroads at the time *Scholarship Reconsidered* was initially published. In what ways, if at all, is higher education at a comparable crossroads today?
2. What did Boyer mean when he argued for the legitimacy of the full range of scholarship?
3. Why did Boyer's work catch the attention of higher education reformers? What might it offer to the current generation of voices calling for reform?

The Origins of *Scholarship Reconsidered*

1. In what ways did the ethos of *Scholarship Reconsidered* reflect components of Boyer's own life story? The characteristics of the institutions he served?
2. In what ways did the results of the surveys Boyer and his colleagues conducted reveal a sense of dissonance between what faculty members valued and how they were rewarded? Does such a sense of dissonance persist to this day?
3. What were the primary criticisms of *Scholarship Reconsidered*? Do you agree with any of those criticisms? If so, in what ways?

Boyer's Impact on Faculty Development

1. What constitutes faculty development as a professional endeavor? In what ways, if at all, have you benefited from efforts led by such colleagues? In what ways could such efforts be improved?
2. How did the maturation of faculty development programs benefit from the publication of *Scholarship Reconsidered*? From the scholarship of teaching and learning (SoTL)?
3. Andrea L. Beach argued that the resources found in *Scholarship Reconsidered* and defined as SoTL are even more critical today. Why does she make that argument? Given the needs of your campus community, do you agree? Disagree? Why?

The Influence of *Scholarship Reconsidered* on Institutional Types and Academic Disciplines

1. John M. Braxton offered that Boyer put forth three assertions in *Scholarship Reconsidered*. What were those assertions?
2. According to Braxton, how has the application of the themes in *Scholarship Reconsidered* varied by type of institution? By discipline?
3. In your particular institutional and disciplinary context, what potentially are the greatest points of applicability offered by *Scholarship Reconsidered*? Disconnect?

Scholarship Reconsidered's Impact on Doctoral and Professional Education

1. In what ways, if any, were ideas from reports such as *Scholarship Reconsidered* implicit in your doctoral and/or professional education? If not, in what ways, if at all, might such ideas have improved it?
2. In what ways is education in the professions changing? Expected to change in the future? In what ways might the ideas in *Scholarship Reconsidered* prove to be ongoing resources?
3. In particular, how can *Scholarship Reconsidered* be a resource in preparing the next generation of scholars and practitioners?

How *Scholarship Reconsidered* Disrupted the Promotion and Tenure System

1. In your opinion, is *Scholarship Reconsidered* an argument for faculty members who cannot do the work of traditional scholars? If so, why? If not, why not?
2. In what ways has *Scholarship Reconsidered* affected how faculty members are evaluated? In what ways has its influence fallen short of its original intentions?
3. Given your particular institutional and disciplinary contexts, in what ways could *Scholarship Reconsidered* prove helpful in a revision of promotion and tenure requirements? Unhelpful?

Chapter One

1. What were the competing obligations posing challenges to institutions at the time *Scholarship Reconsidered* was initially published? What, if any, are the competing challenges facing institutions today?
2. How do you define a scholar? What qualities define such a person? What practices demand his or her attention?
3. In what ways, if any, does your institution serve a larger community (or larger set of communities)? If so, what larger community (or communities) does it serve?
4. In your disciplinary context, is it difficult for a person to secure tenure if he or she does not produce scholarly work? Why? Why not?
5. Boyer argued that as higher education was becoming more inclusive, the professoriate was becoming more hierarchical and restrictive. Is such a transition problematic? If so, why? Or is such a transition the logical result of the evolution of a profession?

Chapter Two

1. What is basic research? How has its definition changed over the course of the last fifty years? Twenty-five years?
2. Should scholarship be viewed as more than research? If so, why? If not, why not?

3. What does Boyer mean when he writes that the probing mind of the scholar is an incalculably vital asset to the academy and the world? How do institutional communities cultivate such qualities of the mind? Damage such qualities?
4. How does Boyer define the scholarship of discovery, integration, application (engagement), and teaching? Which one of these forms of scholarship is most highly valued in your particular institutional and disciplinary context? Why? Least highly valued? Why?

Chapter Three

1. When it comes to the production of scholarship, how far should the range of faculty scholarship be extended? In essence, should there be some parameters? If so, how should those parameters be set?
2. Does the definition of scholarship currently in place in your institutional and disciplinary contexts value textbook writing? Popular writing? If so, why? If not, why not?
3. How is scholarship assessed in your institutional and disciplinary contexts? In what ways, if any, does it succeed in meeting the needs of members of those communities? In what ways, if any, can it be improved?
4. Who is involved in that assessment process? In what ways are those individuals involved? Should they be involved? Should others be involved?
5. Does your institutional and disciplinary context employ the practice of developing a portfolio? If so, how are such portfolios designed? Is their design too expansive? If so, why? Too restrictive? If so, why?

Chapter Four

1. In your present role, do you feel more affected by forces of stagnation and/or generativity? In what ways, if at all, do your institutional and disciplinary contexts contribute to such feelings?
2. Do you and/or your colleagues face stress and burnout realities? If so, why? How might such pressures change over time (for assistant professors, associate professors, full professors, etc.)?
3. What practices could lead to the renewal of faculty member energy and focus? If needed, how could such practices be incorporated in your institution? In your discipline?

4. What is your assessment of what Boyer identifies as creativity contracts? Do your institutional and disciplinary contexts currently employ a form of such contracts? If so, how? If not, do you think the incorporation of some form of such contracts might prove to be of some benefit? If so, how?
5. How can such contracts reflect a wide range of talents while still meeting the needs of institutional and disciplinary contexts?

Chapter Five

1. What goals are most central to your institutional community? How were those goals cultivated? Communicated?
2. Are those goals appropriately unique to your institution? If so, in what ways? If not, what pressures have kept your campus from developing such a sense of identity?
3. What role, if any, do interdisciplinary institutes and programs play on your campus in terms of the cultivation of scholarship?
4. In what ways, if at all, might collaboration with other inter-institutional and extra-institutional colleagues be of benefit to you in terms of the practice of scholarship?
5. In what ways should the practice of scholarship be tailored to particular institutional needs? Disciplinary needs? Individual needs?

Chapter Six

1. What does Boyer mean when he argued that tomorrow's scholars must be liberally educated? Did that happen over the course of the last twenty-five years? Is it happening today?
2. Is the quality of training that scholars receive through their graduate work and then on into professional development programs offered by their institutional and disciplinary contexts suitable for the work they are called on to conduct? If so, why? If not, why not and what can be done to improve it?
3. What is your assessment of the value of the dissertation and the role it plays in forming the next generation of scholars? In what ways, if any, could such a practice be improved?
4. Was teaching sufficiently emphasized in your graduate experience? Particular institutional and disciplinary context? If not, what could be done to improve it?

5. Or, is teaching overemphasized in your particular institutional and disciplinary context? If so, how much room does such an emphasis leave for the practice of scholarship? Service? What can be done to offer faculty members a more evenly distributed set of professional development offerings?

Chapter Seven

1. Boyer argued that he strongly affirmed the importance of research—the scholarship of discovery. Now that you have read the whole text, do you think he accomplished such a goal? If so, why? Or was the introduction of the scholarship of discovery, integration, application (engagement), and teaching simply an argument for faculty members who cannot do the work of traditional scholars?
2. In what ways can faculty member obligations be reasonably extended beyond the classroom? In essence, what vital roles can faculty members play both on their campuses and in their respective communities?
3. According to Boyer, what kinds of scholars does academe need? Society need? What changes, if any, need to be made in relation to the academic vocation in order to align it with such needs?
4. If needed, how can faculty members in your particular institutional and disciplinary contexts assume responsibility for giving scholarship a richer, more vital meaning?
5. In what ways, if at all, should the practice of scholarship bring faculty members together? What are the ramifications for how scholarship is proposed, funded, generated, and assessed?

Afterword

1. What kind of work, if at all, needs to be done today to bring validity to the wide-ranging span of academic work?
2. Do your particular institutional and disciplinary contexts face confusion in terms of defining and assessing scholarship? Would *Scholarship Reconsidered* alleviate such confusion? Increase such confusion?
3. In what ways, if at all, can *Scholarship Reconsidered* serve as a means of reinforcing the unique institutional and disciplinary contexts in which you conduct your work?

NOTES

Foreword

1. E. L. Boyer, *Scholarship Reconsidered: Priorities of the Professoriate* (Princeton, NJ: Carnegie Foundation for the Advancement of Teaching, 1990), 16.
2. C. E. Glassick, M. T. Huber, and G. I. Maeroff, *Scholarship Assessed: Evaluation of the Professoriate* (San Francisco: Jossey-Bass, 1997).
3. M.T. Huber and P. Hutchings, *The Advancement of Learning: Building the Teaching Commons* (San Francisco: Jossey-Bass, 2005); P. Hutchings, M. T. Huber, and A. Ciccone, *The Scholarship of Teaching and Learning Reconsidered: Institutional Integration and Impact* (San Francisco: Jossey-Bass, 2011).
4. Boyer, *Scholarship Reconsidered,* 16.
5. Ibid.

Part One

The Origins of *Scholarship Reconsidered*

1. E. L. Boyer, *Scholarship Reconsidered: Priorities of the Professoriate* (Princeton, NJ: Carnegie Foundation for the Advancement of Teaching, 1990).

2. The Carnegie Foundation for the Advancement of Teaching, *Campus Life: In Search of Community*; with a foreword by Ernest L. Boyer (Lawrenceville, NJ: Princeton University Press, 1990).
3. Boyer, *Scholarship Reconsidered,* 16.
4. A. D. Bloom, *The Closing of the American Mind: How Higher Education Has Failed Democracy and Impoverished the Souls of Today's Students* (New York: Simon and Schuster, 1987).
5. G. H. Holland, "Interview of Grace Herr Holland/Interviewer: Merle Brubacher" (Box T02, Folder 01) (Mechanicsburg, PA: The Ernest L. Boyer Center, Messiah College, 2004).
6. E. L. Boyer, "Excellence in Education" [Paper delivered at the 1990 Commencement at the University of Utah, Salt Lake City, UT, June 11, 1993] (Catalog No.: 1000 0001 2903, The Ernest L. Boyer, Sr. Archives Collection) (Mechanicsburg, PA: The Ernest L. Boyer Center, Messiah College, 1993), 3.
7. J. Z. Martin, "Interview of John Z. Martin/Interviewer: Merle Brubacher" (Box T02, Folder 01) (Mechanicsburg, PA: The Ernest L. Boyer Center, Messiah College, 2004).
8. H. Edelman, "ESC 2.0 Leading the Future of Higher Education" (Fall 2014). www.esc.edu/connections/fall-2014/esc-20.html.
9. E. L. Boyer and A. Levine, *A Quest for Common Learning: The Aims of General Education* (Washington, DC: Carnegie Foundation for the Advancement of Teaching, 1981); E. L. Boyer, *High School: A Report on Secondary Education in America* (New York: Harper & Row, 1983); E. L. Boyer, *College: The Undergraduate Experience in America* (Princeton, NJ: Carnegie Foundation for the Advancement of Teaching, 1987); The Carnegie Foundation for the Advancement of Teaching, *Campus Life.*
10. E. L. Boyer, "The New American Scholar" [Paper delivered at the 1990 National Conference of the American Association of Higher Education, San Francisco, CA, April 1, 1990] (Catalog No.: 1000 0001 0302, The Ernest L. Boyer, Sr. Archives Collection) (Mechanicsburg, PA: The Ernest L. Boyer Center, Messiah College, 1990).
11. C. E. Glassick, "Boyer's Expanded Definitions of Scholarship, the Standards for Assessing Scholarship, and the Elusiveness of the Scholarship of Teaching," *Academic Medicine,* vol. 75, no. 9 (2000), 877–880.
12. Ibid.
13. Ibid, 878.
14. Glassick, "Boyer's Expanded Definitions of Scholarship, the Standards for Assessing Scholarship, and the Elusiveness of the Scholarship of Teaching."

15. E. L. Boyer, "The Scholarship of Engagement" [Paper delivered at the 1995 Induction Ceremony of the American Academy of Arts and Sciences, Somerville, MA, October 11, 1995] (Catalog No.: 1000 0001 5872, The Ernest L. Boyer, Sr. Archives Collection) (Mechanicsburg, PA: The Ernest L. Boyer Center, Messiah College, 1995), 88.
16. E. L. Boyer, "Rationality and Morality in Higher Education" [Paper delivered at 1980 Regional Conference of the Danforth Associates, Yosemite, CA, February 8, 1908] (Catalog No.: 1000 0000 1267, The Ernest L. Boyer, Sr. Archives Collection) (Mechanicsburg, PA: The Ernest L. Boyer Center, Messiah College, 1980); E. L. Boyer, "A College of Quality" [Paper Delivered at 74th Annual Meeting of the Association of American Colleges, Washington, DC, January 14, 1988] (Catalog No.: 1000 0000 3704, The Ernest L. Boyer, Sr. Archives Collection) (Mechanicsburg, PA: The Ernest L. Boyer Center, Messiah College, 1988).
17. G. R. Bucher and J. J. Patton, "What Would Boyer Do?" *About Campus,* vol. 9, no. 2 (2004), 3.
18. Ibid.
19. Glassick, "Boyer's Expanded Definitions of Scholarship, the Standards for Assessing Scholarship, and the Elusiveness of the Scholarship of Teaching," 877.
20. Ibid., 878.
21. K. Bruns, N. Conklin, M. Wright, D. Hoover, B. Brace, G. Wise, and ... J. Childers, "Scholarship: The Key to Creating Change through Outreach," *Journal of Higher Education Outreach and Engagement,* vol. 8, no. 1 (2003), 3–11.
22. M. Fiddler, S. McGury, C. Marienau, R. Rogers, and W. Scheideman, "Broadening the Scope of Scholarship: A Suggested Framework," *Innovative Higher Education,* vol. 21, no. 2 (1996), 138.
23. S. G. Estes, "Introduction: Beyond *Scholarship Reconsidered,*" *Quest,* vol. 48 (1996), 128.
24. M. B. Paulsen and K. A. Feldman, "Toward a Reconceptualization of Scholarship: A Human Action System with Functional Imperatives," *Journal of Higher Education,* vol. 66 (1995), 615–640.
25. A. W. McNeil, "Reflections on *Scholarship Reconsidered,*" *Quest,* vol. 48 (1996), 143.
26. A. M. Rubin, "Is Boyer Misguided or Misused? The Scholarship of Confusion," *Journal of the Association for Communication Administration,* vol. 29 (2000), 263.
27. Ibid.

28. Glassick, "Boyer's Expanded Definitions of Scholarship, the Standards for Assessing Scholarship, and the Elusiveness of the Scholarship of Teaching."
29. R. D. Simpson, "Toward a Scholarship of Outreach and Engagement in Higher Education," *Journal of Higher Education Outreach and Engagement*, vol. 6, no. 1 (2000), 7–12.

Boyer's Impact on Faculty Development

1. E. L. Boyer, *Scholarship Reconsidered: Priorities of the Professoriate* (Princeton, NJ: Carnegie Foundation for the Advancement of Teaching, 1990), 23.
2. For example, C. E. Glassick, M. T. Huber, and G. I. Maeroff, *Scholarship Assessed: Evaluation of the Professoriate* (San Francisco: Jossey-Bass, 1997); P. Hutchings and L. S. Shulman, "The Scholarship of Teaching: New Elaborations, New Developments," *Change: The Magazine of Higher Learning*, vol. 31, no. 5 (1999), 10–15.
3. P. Hutchings, M. T. Huber, and A. Cicconne, *The Scholarship of Teaching and Learning Reconsidered: Institutional Integration and Impact* (San Francisco: Jossey Bass, 2011).
4. J. North and S. C. Scholl, "POD: The Founding of a National Network," *POD Quarterly*, vol. 1, no. 1 (1979), 10–17; L. Ortquist-Ahrens, "Thriving in the 21st Century," Presidential Address, 39th Annual Conference of the Professional and Organizational Development Network in Higher Education, Dallas (November 6, 2014).
5. M. D. Sorcinelli, A. E. Austin, P. L. Eddy, and A. L. Beach, *Creating the Future of Faculty Development: Learning from the Past, Understanding the Present* (Bolton, MA: Anker Publishing, 2006).
6. For example, National Commission on Excellence in Education (1983). *A Nation at Risk: The Imperative for Educational Reform.* A report to the nation and the Secretary of Education. United States Department of Education. Washington, D.C.; Study Group on the Conditions of Excellence in American Higher Education (1984). *Involvement in Learning: Realizing the Potential of American Higher Education.* Washington DC: National Institute of Education.
7. E. L. Boyer, *College: The Undergraduate Experience in America* (New York: Harper & Row, 1987).
8. Sorcinelli, Austin, Eddy, and Beach, *Creating the Future of Faculty Development.*

9. Hutchings, Huber, and Cicconne, *The Scholarship of Teaching and Learning Reconsidered.*
10. L. Richlin, "The Ongoing Cycle of Scholarly Teaching and the Scholarship of Teaching," Paper presented at the 13th annual Lilly Conference on College and University Teaching, Oxford, OH (November 1993); M. D. Cox, "The Development of New and Junior Faculty," in *Teaching Improvement Practices: Successful Strategies for Higher Education,* W. A. Wright and Associates, eds. (Bolton, MA: Anker, 1995), 283–310.
11. W. A. Wright and M. C. O'Neill, "Teaching Improvement Practices: New Perspectives," *To Improve the Academy,* vol. 13 (1994), 5–38.
12. For example, M. D. Cox, "Faculty Learning Communities: Change Agents for Transforming Institutions into Learning Organizations," *To Improve the Academy,* vol. 19 (2001), 69–93; M. D. Cox, "Fostering the Scholarship of Teaching and Learning through Faculty Learning Communities," *Journal on Excellence in College Teaching,* vo. 14, no. 2/3 (2003), 161–198; M. D. Cox, "Introduction to Faculty Learning Communities," in *Building Faculty Learning Communities,* M. D. Cox and L. Richlin, eds. (New Directions for Teaching and Learning, no. 97) (San Francisco: Jossey-Bass, 2004), 5-23; (Richlin & Cox, 2004).
13. L. Richlin and A. Essington, "Overview of Faculty Learning Communities," in *Building Faculty Learning Communities,* M. D. Cox and L. Richlin, eds. (New Directions for Teaching and Learning, no. 97) (San Francisco: Jossey-Bass, 2004), 25–40.
14. A. L. Beach and M. D. Cox, "The Impact of Faculty Learning Communities on Teaching and Learning," *Learning Communities Journal,* vol. 1 (2009), 7–27.
15. Boyer, *Scholarship Reconsidered.*
16. Sorcinelli, Austin, Eddy, and Beach, *Creating the Future of Faculty Development.*
17. A. L. Beach, M. D. Sorcinelli, A. E. Austin, and J. K. Rivard, *Faculty Development in the Age of Evidence* (Sterling, VA: Stylus Publishing, forthcoming).
18. Beach, Sorcinelli, Austin, and Rivard, *Faculty Development in the Age of Evidence*; Sorcinelli, Austin, Eddy, and Beach, *Creating the Future of Faculty Development.*
19. CIRTL Network, "Teaching-as-Research" (n.d.) www.cirtl.net/CoreIdeas/teaching_as_research.
20. B. A. Fischer, M. D. Repice, C. L. Dufault, D. F. Leonard, and R. F. Frey, "Developing Scholarly Teachers through an SoTL Faculty Fellowship," *To Improve the Academy,* vol. 33, no. 2, (2014), 175–195.

21. A. L. Beach, M. D. Sorcinelli, A. E. Austin, and J. K. Rivard, "Faculty Development 2020: A Forecast and Guide to the Years Ahead," POD Annual Conference (November 6, 2014); Beach, Sorcinelli, Austin, and Rivard, *Faculty Development in the Age of Evidence.*

The Influence of *Scholarship Reconsidered* on Institutional Types and Academic Disciplines

1. T. Parsons and G. M. Platt. *The American University* (Cambridge, MA: Harvard University Press, 1973); John M. Braxton and William Toombs, "Faculty Uses of Doctoral Training: Consideration of a Technique for the Differentiation of a Scholarly Effort from Research Activity," *Research in Higher Education,* vol. 16, no. 3 (1982), 265–282.
2. R. T. Blackburn and J. H. Lawrence, *Faculty at Work: Motivation, Expectation, Satisfaction* (Baltimore, MD: Johns Hopkins University Press, 1995); M. Fox, "Publication, Performance, and Reward in Science and Scholarship," in *Higher Education: Handbook of Theory and Research* (vol. 1), J. C. Smart, ed. (New York: Agathon Press, 1985), 255–282.
3. J. M. Braxton and L. Hargens, "Variation among Academic Disciplines: Analytical Frameworks and Research," in *Higher Education: Handbook of Theory and Research* (vol. 11), J. C. Smart, ed. (New York: Agathon Press, 1996), 1–46.
4. J. W. Creswell, *Faculty Research Performance: Lessons from the Sciences and Social Sciences* (Washington, DC: Association for the Study of Higher Education, 1985); Blackburn and Lawrence, *Faculty at Work.*
5. Braxton and Hargens, "Variation among Academic Disciplines."
6. E. L. Boyer, *Scholarship Reconsidered: Priorities of the Professoriate* (Princeton, NJ: Carnegie Foundation for the Advancement of Teaching, 1990).
7. Ibid.
8. L. Shulman and P. Hutchings, *About the Scholarship of Teaching and Learning* (Menlo Park, CA: The Carnegie Foundation for the Advancement of Teaching, 1998).
9. J. M. Braxton, W. Luckey, and P. Helland, *Institutionalizing a Broader View of Scholarship through Boyer's Four Domains* (San Francisco: Jossey-Bass, 2002).
10. Ibid.
11. J. M. Braxton and D. Lyken-Segosebe, "Community College Faculty Engagement in Boyer Domains of Scholarship," in *Community College*

Faculty Scholarship, J. M. Braxton, ed. (New Directions for Community Colleges) (San Francisco: Jossey-Bass, in press).

12. Braxton, Luckey, and Helland, *Institutionalizing a Broader View of Scholarship through Boyer's Four Domains.*
13. Braxton and Lyken-Segosebe, "Community College Faculty Engagement in Boyer Domains of Scholarship."
14. Braxton, Luckey, and Helland, *Institutionalizing a Broader View of Scholarship through Boyer's Four Domains.*
15. Braxton and Lyken-Segosebe, "Community College Faculty Engagement in Boyer Domains of Scholarship."
16. Braxton, Luckey, and Helland, *Institutionalizing a Broader View of Scholarship through Boyer's Four Domains.*
17. Braxton and Lyken-Segosebe, "Community College Faculty Engagement in Boyer Domains of Scholarship."
18. Braxton, Luckey, and Helland, *Institutionalizing a Broader View of Scholarship through Boyer's Four Domains.*
19. Braxton and Lyken-Segosebe, "Community College Faculty Engagement in Boyer Domains of Scholarship."
20. Braxton, Luckey, and Helland, *Institutionalizing a Broader View of Scholarship through Boyer's Four Domains.*
21. Ibid.
22. Braxton and Lyken-Segosebe, "Community College Faculty Engagement in Boyer Domains of Scholarship."
23. Braxton, Luckey, and Helland, *Institutionalizing a Broader View of Scholarship through Boyer's Four Domains.*
24. Ibid.
25. Ibid.
26. Ibid.
27. Braxton and Lyken-Segosebe, "Community College Faculty Engagement in Boyer Domains of Scholarship."
28. Ibid.; Braxton, Luckey, and Helland, *Institutionalizing a Broader View of Scholarship through Boyer's Four Domains.*
29. Boyer, *Scholarship Reconsidered.*
30. Ibid.
31. Ibid., 57.
32. Ibid., 57–58.

33. Braxton, Luckey, and Helland, *Institutionalizing a Broader View of Scholarship through Boyer's Four Domains.*
34. Boyer, *Scholarship Reconsidered,* 58.
35. Braxton, Luckey, and Helland, *Institutionalizing a Broader View of Scholarship through Boyer's Four Domains.*
36. Ibid.
37. Ibid.
38. Boyer, *Scholarship Reconsidered.*
39. Braxton, Luckey, and Helland, *Institutionalizing a Broader View of Scholarship through Boyer's Four Domains.*
40. Boyer, *Scholarship Reconsidered,* 59.
41. Ibid.
42. Ibid., 60.
43. Braxton and Lyken-Segosebe, "Community College Faculty Engagement in Boyer Domains of Scholarship."
44. Boyer, *Scholarship Reconsidered.*
45. O. Fulton and M. Trow, "Research Activity in American Higher Education," *Sociology of Education,* vol. 47 (1974), 29–73; M. J. Finkelstein, *The American Academic Profession: A Synthesis of Social Scientific Inquiry since World War II* (Columbus: Ohio State University Press, 1984); Creswell, *Faculty Research Performance*; Blackburn and Lawrence, *Faculty at Work: Motivation, Expectation, Satisfaction.*
46. Braxton and Hargens, "Variation among Academic Disciplines."
47. A. Biglan, "Relationships between Subject Matter Characteristics and the Structure and Output of University Departments," *Journal of Applied Psychology,* vol. 57, no. 3 (1973), 204–213.
48. J. M. Braxton and M. Del Favero, "Evaluating Scholarship Performance: Traditional and Emergent Assessment Templates," in *Evaluating Faculty Performance,* C. L. Colbeck, ed. (New Directions for Institutional Research, vol. 114) (San Francisco: Jossey-Bass, 2002).
49. Boyer, *Scholarship Reconsidered.*

Scholarship Reconsidered's Impact on Doctoral and Professional Education

1. A. Kezar and C. Sam, "Understanding the New Majority of Non-Tenure-Track Faculty in Higher Education: Demographics, Experiences, and Plans of Action," *ASHE Higher Education Series,* vol. 36, no. 4 (2010) (San Francisco: Jossey-Bass); J. H. Schuster and M. J. Finkelstein, *The American Faculty: The Restructuring of Academic Work and Careers* (Baltimore: Johns Hopkins University Press, 2006).

2. D. M. Irby, M. Cooke, and B. C. O'Brien, "Calls for Reform of Medical Education by the Carnegie Foundation for the Advancement of Teaching: 1910–2010," *Academic Medicine,* no. 85, no. 2 (2010), 220–227.
3. American Bar Association, "Report and Recommendations: Task Force on the Future of Legal Education" (2013), 13. www.americanbar.org/content/dam/aba/administrative/professional_responsibility/report_and_recommendations_of_aba_task_force.authcheckdam.pdf.
4. A. E. Austin, "Preparing the Next Generation of Faculty: Graduate Education as Socialization to the Academic Career," *The Journal of Higher Education,* vol. 73, no. 2 (2002), 94–122; J. M. Gappa, A. E. Austin, and A. G. Trice, *Rethinking Faculty Work: Higher Education's Strategic Imperative* (San Francisco: Jossey-Bass, 2007).
5. E. L. Boyer, *Scholarship Reconsidered: Priorities of the Professoriate* (Princeton, NJ: Carnegie Foundation for the Advancement of Teaching, 1990), 53.
6. Ibid., 57.
7. Committee on Science, Engineering, and Public Policy (COSEPUP) of the National Academies of Sciences, The National Academies of Engineering, and the Institute of Medicine, *Reshaping the Graduate Education of Scientists and Engineers* (Washington, DC: National Academy Press, 1995); Council of Graduate School's Advisory Committee on Graduate Education and American Competitiveness, *Graduate Education: The Backbone of American Competitiveness and Innovation* (Washington, DC: Council of Graduate Schools (2007); National Science Board, *The Science and Engineering Workforce: Realizing America's Potential* (NSB 03-69) (Washington, DC: National Science Foundation, 2003); National Science Board, *Science and Engineering Indicators 2006* (vols. 1 and 2) (Arlington, VA: National Science Foundation, 2006); G. E. Walker, C. M. Golde, L. Jones, A. C. Bueschel, and P. Hutchings, *The Formation of Scholars: Rethinking Doctoral Education for the Twenty-First Century* (San Francisco: Jossey-Bass, 2008).
8. J. Welch Wegner, "The Carnegie Foundation's Educating Lawyers: Four Questions for Bar Examiners," *The Bar Examiner,* vol. 80, no. 2 (2011), 11–24.
9. C. E. Glassick, M. T. Huber, and G. I. Maeroff, *Scholarship Assessed: Evaluation of the Professoriate* (San Francisco: Jossey-Bass, 1997).
10. Walker, Golde, Jones, Bueschel, and Hutchings, *The Formation of Scholars,* 8.
11. Boyer, *Scholarship Reconsidered.*

How *Scholarship Reconsidered* Disrupted the Promotion and Tenure System

1. E. L. Boyer, *Scholarship Reconsidered: Priorities of the Professoriate* (Princeton, NJ: Carnegie Foundation for the Advancement of Teaching, 1990).
2. E. L. Boyer, "The Scholarship of Engagement," *Journal of Public Outreach,* vol. 1, no. 1 (1996), 11–20; C. E. Glassick, M. T. Huber, and G. I. Maeroff, *Scholarship Assessed: Evaluation of the Professoriate* (San Francisco: Jossey-Bass, 1997).
3. J. M. Braxton, W. Luckey, and P. Helland, "Ideal and Actual Value Patterns toward Domains of Scholarship in Three Types of Colleges and Universities," in *Analyzing Work and Rewards: Using Boyer's Four Domains of Scholarship,* J. Braxton, ed. (New Directions for Institutional Research, vol. 129) (San Francisco: Jossey-Bass, 2006), 67–77; K. O'Meara and R. E. Rice, eds., *Faculty Priorities Reconsidered: Encouraging Multiple Forms of Scholarship* (San Francisco: Jossey-Bass, 2005); K. O'Meara, "Encouraging Multiple Forms of Scholarship in Faculty Reward Systems: Does It Make a Difference?" *Research in Higher Education,* vol. 46, no. 5 (2005), 479–510; K. O'Meara, "Encouraging Multiple Forms of Scholarship in Faculty Reward Systems: Have Academic Cultures Really Changed? in *Analyzing Work and Rewards: Using Boyer's Four Domains of Scholarship,* J. Braxton, ed. (New Directions for Institutional Research, vol. 129) (San Francisco: Jossey-Bass, 2006), 77–96; K. O'Meara, "Encouraging Multiple Forms of Scholarship in Faculty Reward Systems: Influence on Faculty Work Life," *Planning for Higher Education,* vol. 34, no. 2 (2006), 43–53.
4. Braxton, Luckey, and Helland, "Ideal and Actual Value Patterns toward Domains of Scholarship in Three Types of Colleges and Universities," 74.
5. K. O'Meara, "Inside the Panopticon: Studying Academic Reward Systems," in *Higher Education: Handbook of Theory and Research* (vol. 26), J. C. Smart and M. B. Paulsen, eds. (New York: Springer, 2011), 161–220.
6. K. O'Meara, "Faculty Civic Engagement: New Training, Assumptions, and Markets Needed for the Engaged American Scholar," in *To Serve a Larger Purpose: Engagement for Democracy and the Transformation of Higher Education,* J. Saltmarsh and M. Hartley, eds. (Philadelphia: Temple University Press, 2011), 177–198.
7. L. D. Gonzales, "Faculty Sense-Making and Mission Creep: Interrogating Institutionalized Ways of Knowing and Doing Legitimacy," *Review of Higher Education,* vol. 36, no. 2 (2013), 179–209; O'Meara, "Inside the Panopticon"; D. A. Schön, *"The New Scholarship Requires a New Epistemology," Change,* vol. 27, no. 6 (1995), 26–34.

8. K. O'Meara, "Scholarship Unbound: Assessing Service as Scholarship for Promotion and Tenure," in *Studies in Higher Education Dissertation Series,* P. G. Altbach, ed. (New York: Routledge, 2002).
9. O'Meara and Rice, *Faculty Priorities Reconsidered.*
10. O'Meara, "Encouraging Multiple Forms of Scholarship in Faculty Reward Systems" (2005); O'Meara, "Encouraging Multiple Forms of Scholarship in Faculty Reward Systems" (2006); O'Meara, "Encouraging Multiple Forms of Scholarship in Faculty Reward Systems" (2006).
11. O'Meara, "Encouraging Multiple Forms of Scholarship in Faculty Reward Systems" (2006); O'Meara, "Encouraging Multiple Forms of Scholarship in Faculty Reward Systems" (2006).
12. Ibid.
13. E. A. Lynton, *Making the Case for Professional Service* (Washington, DC: American Association for Higher Education, 1995).
14. R. Chait, ed., *The Questions of Tenure* (Cambridge, MA: Harvard University Press, 2002).
15. O'Meara and Rice, *Faculty Priorities Reconsidered.*
16. W. R. Scott, *Institutions and Organizations* (Thousand Oaks, CA: Sage, 1995), 45.
17. M. N. Bastedo and N. A. Bowman, "College Rankings as an Inter-Organizational Dependency: Establishing the Foundation for Strategic and Institutional Accounts," *Research in Higher Education,* vol. 52, no. 1 (2011), 3–23; B. J. Taylor and C. C. Morphew, "An Analysis of Baccalaureate College Mission Statements," *Research in Higher Education,* vol. 51, no. 5 (2010), 483–503.
18. J. Saltmarsh and E. Zlotkowski, *Higher Education and Democracy: Essays on Service-Learning and Civic Engagement* (Philadelphia: Temple University Press, 2011).
19. R. E. Rice, *Making a Place for the New American Scholar* (Working Paper Series) (Washington, DC: American Association for Higher Education, 1996).
20. K. O'Meara, "Faculty Civic Engagement," 177–198.
21. J. Blackmore and J. Sachs, *Performing and Reforming Leaders: Gender, Educational Restructuring, and Organizational Change* (Albany: SUNY Press, 2007).
22. Ibid.
23. C. Jencks and D. Riesman, *The Academic Revolution* (Garden City, NY: Doubleday, 1968).
24. Boyer, *Scholarship Reconsidered*; Boyer, "The Scholarship of Engagement."

25. R. B. Barr and J. Tagg, "From Teaching to Learning: A New Paradigm for Undergraduate Education," *Change: The Magazine of Higher Learning*, vol. 27, no. 6 (1995), 12–26.
26. Boyer, *Scholarship Reconsidered.*
27. O'Meara, 2011; K. O'Meara and M. Meekins, *Inside Rankings: Limitations and Possibilities* (Working Paper, 2012 Series, no. 1) (Boston: New England Resource Center for Higher Education, 2012).
28. Gonzales, "Faculty Sense-Making and Mission Creep"; K. O'Meara, "Striving for What? Exploring the Pursuit of Prestige," in *Higher Education: Handbook of Theory and Research* (vol. 22), J. Smart, ed. (New York: Springer, 2007), 121–179; K. O'Meara and A. Bloomgarden, "The Pursuit of Prestige: Examining the Consequences of Striving for Faculty Work-Life, Reward Systems, and Satisfaction," *Journal of the Professoriate*, vol. 4, no. 1 (2010), 40–74.
29. C. Orphan and J. Saltmarsh, "Collaborative Futures: Critical Reflections on Publicly Active Graduate Education," *eJournal of Public Affairs*, vol. 2, no. 2 (2013). http://ejournal.missouristate.edu/2013/08/collaborative-futures/.
30. T. Eatman, "The Arc of the Academic Career Bends toward Publicly Engaged Scholarship," in *Collaborative Futures: Critical Reflections on Publicly Active Graduate Education*, A. Gilvin, C. Martin, and G. M. Roberts, eds. (Syracuse, NY: Syracuse University Graduate School Press, 2012), 25–48.

Part Two

Scholarship Over Time

1. Ernest L. Boyer, *College: The Undergraduate Experience in America* (New York: Harper & Row, 1987), 131.
2. Donald Kennedy, "Stanford in Its Second Century," address to the Stanford community, Stanford University, at the meeting of the Academic Council (April 5, 1990).
3. University of California, "Lower Division Education in the University of California," *A Report from the Task Force on Lower Division Education* (June 1986).
4. The University of Pennsylvania, *A Handbook for Faculty and Academic Administrators: A Selection of Policies and Procedures of the University of Pennsylvania* (1989), 40.

5. Robert Gavin, convocation speech, Macalester College (September 13, 1990).
6. From "New England's First Fruits," a description of the founding of Harvard College, in *Turning Points in American Educational History,* David B. Tyack, ed. (New York: John Wiley & Sons, 1967), 2.
7. Theodore M. Benditt, "The Research Demands of Teaching in Modem Higher Education," in *Morality, Responsibility, and the University: Studies in Academic Ethics,* Steven M. Cahn, ed. (Philadelphia: Temple University Press, 1990), 94.
8. Charles W. Eliot, *Educational Reform: Essays and Addresses* (New York: Century, 1898), 27; Walter P. Metzger, "The Academic Profession in the United States," in *The Academic Profession: National, Disciplinary, & Institutional Settings,* Burton R. Clark, ed. (Berkeley: The University of California Press, 1987), 135.
9. Frederick Rudolph, *The American College and University: A History* (New York: Alfred A. Knopf, 1962), 48–49.
10. Ibid., 229.
11. Rudolph, *The American College and University,* 231; citing William Lathrop Kingsley, ed., *Yale College: A Sketch of Its History* (vol. I) (New York, 1879), 150–152.
12. Rudolph, *The American College and University,* 65; citing Henry Adams, *The Education of Henry Adams* (Boston, 1918), 305–306.
13. Willa Cather, *My Antonia* (Boston: Houghton Mifflin, 1954), 258.
14. David Starr Jordon, *The Voice of the Scholar* (San Francisco: P. Elder and Co., 1903), 46; in Laurence R. Veysey, *The Emergence of the American University* (Chicago: The University of Chicago Press, 1965), 61.
15. Charles W. Eliot, *University Administration* (Boston, Houghton Mifflin Company 1908), 227–228; in Veysey, *The Emergence of the American University,* 119.
16. Veysey, *The Emergence of the American University,* 63; quoting Ezra Cornell, "Address," in Cornell University, *Register* (1869–1870), 17.
17. Ernest L. Boyer and Fred M. Hechinger, *Higher Learning in the Nation's Service* (Washington, DC: Carnegie Foundation for the Advancement of Teaching, 1981), 12.
18. Ralph Waldo Emerson, *The Collected Works of Ralph Waldo Emerson, Volume 1: Nature, Addresses, and Lectures,* introductions and notes by Robert E. Spiller, text established by Alfred R. Ferguson (Cambridge, MA: The Belknap Press of Harvard University Press, 1971), 59.
19. Boyer and Hechinger, *Higher Learning in the Nation's Service,* 13.

20. Lincoln Steffens, "Sending a State to College," *American Magazine* (February 1909); reprinted in *Portraits of the American University 1890–1910,* James C. Stone and Donald P. DeNevi, comps. (San Francisco: Jossey-Bass, 1971), 133.
21. Margaret Rossiter, "The Organization of the Agricultural Sciences," in *The Organization of Knowledge in Modern America, 1860–1920,* Alexandra Oleson and John Voss, eds. (Baltimore: The Johns Hopkins University Press, 1979), 214.
22. Veysey, *The Emergence of the American University,* 85; citing Andrew D. White to Daniel Coit Gilman (April 12, 1878); and Andrew D. White, *Education in Political Science* (Baltimore, 1879), 22.
23. Edward Shils, "The Order of Learning in the United States: The Ascendancy of the University," in Oleson, A., ed. *The Organization of Knowledge in Modern America,* (Johns Hopkins University Press, 1979), 28.
24. Richard T. Ely to Daniel Coit Gilman (Buchanan, VA, July 11, 1885), D. C. Gilman Papers, Johns Hopkins University, in Thomas L. Haskell, *The Emergence of Professional Social Science: The American Social Science Association and the Nineteenth-Century Crisis of Authority* (Chicago: University of Illinois Press, 1977), 182n.
25. Edwin T. Martin, *Thomas Jefferson, Scientist* (New York: Henry Schuman, 1952), 62.
26. Rudolph, *The American College and University,* 28.
27. Ibid., 118.
28. Dael Wolfle, *The Home of Science: The Role of the University* (Twelfth of a series of profiles sponsored by the Carnegie Commission on Higher Education) (New York: McGraw-Hill, 1972), 5.
29. Wolfle, *The Home of Science,* 5; citing George H. Daniels, *American Science in the Age of Jackson* (New York: Columbia University Press, 1968), 13–14.
30. Jaroslav Pelikan, *Scholarship and Its Survival: Questions on the Idea of Graduate Education* (Princeton, NJ: Carnegie Foundation for the Advancement of Teaching, 1983), 5; citing Edgar S. Furniss, *The Graduate School of Yale: A Brief History* (New Haven, CT: Yale Graduate School, 1965), 24–45.
31. Daniel Fallon, *The German University: A Heroic Ideal in Conflict with the Modern World* (Boulder: Colorado Associated University Press, 1980), 1–3.
32. Ibid., 2–3, citing G. Stanley Hall, "Educational Reforms," *The Pedagogical Seminary* (1892), 6–8.
33. Veysey, *The Emergence of the American University,* 200–201; citing Irving Babbitt, *Literature and the American College* (Boston, 1908), 107–108, 134.

34. Shils, "The Order of Learning in the United States," 28.
35. Pelikan, *Scholarship and Its Survival,* 6.
36. W. H. Cowley, *Presidents, Professors, and Trustees,* ed. Donald T. Williams Jr. (San Francisco: Jossey-Bass, 1981), 160; citing David Starr Jordan, *Report of the Alumni Trustee to the Alumni of Cornell University* (Ithaca, NY: Andrus and Church, 1888), 8–10.
37. Boyer and Hechinger, *Higher Learning in the Nation's Service,* 14.
38. Vannevar Bush, *Science: The Endless Frontier* (Washington, DC: The National Science Foundation, reprinted 1980), 10–11; in Boyer and Hechinger, *Higher Learning in the Nation's Service,* 14–15.
39. Christopher Jencks and David Riesman, *The Academic Revolution* (New York: Doubleday, 1968).
40. Dolores L. Burke, *A New Academic Marketplace* (Westport, CT: Greenwood Press, 1988), 122; citing Theodore Caplow and Reece J. McGee, *The Academic Marketplace* (New York: Basic Books, 1958).
41. The Carnegie Foundation for the Advancement of Teaching (1969) and National Surveys of Faculty (1989).
42. Laurence A. Cremin, *American Education: The Metropolitan Experience, 1876–1980* (New York: Harper & Row, 1988), 251; citing President Harry S. Truman's Commission on Higher Education (1947).
43. Ernest A. Lynton and Sandra E. Elman, *New Priorities for the University* (San Francisco: Jossey-Bass, 1987), 7.

Enlarging the Perspective

1. Charles Wegener, *Liberal Education and the Modern University* (Chicago: The University of Chicago Press, 1978), 9–12; citing Daniel C. Gilman, *The Launching of a University and Other Papers* (New York: Dodd Mead & Co., 1906), 238–239, 242–243.
2. Richard I. Miller, Hongyu Chen, Jerome B. Hart, and Clyde B. Killian, "New Approaches to Faculty Evaluation: A Survey, Initial Report" (Athens, OH, submitted to the Carnegie Foundation for the Advancement of Teaching by Richard I. Miller, professor of higher education, Ohio University, September 4, 1990).
3. William G. Bowen, *Ever the Teacher: William G. Bowen's Writings as President of Princeton* (Princeton, NJ: Princeton University Press, 1987), 269.
4. Harriet Zuckerman, *Scientific Elite: Nobel Laureates in the United States* (New York: The Free Press, 1977), 282–288; citing *The World Book Encyclopedia* (vol. 14) (1975).
5. National Research Council, *Physics through the 1990s* (Washington, DC: National Academy Press, 1986), 8.

6. Lewis Thomas, "Biomedical Science and Human Health: The Long-Range Prospect," *Daedalus* (Spring 1977), 164–169; in Bowen, *Ever the Teacher,* 241–242.
7. Mark Van Doren, *Liberal Education* (Boston: Beacon Press, 1959), 115.
8. Michael Polanyi, *The Tacit Dimension* (Garden City, NY: Doubleday, 1967), 72; in Ernest L. Boyer, *College: The Undergraduate Experience in America* (New York: Harper & Row, 1987), 91.
9. Clifford Geertz, "Blurred Genres: The Refiguration of Social Thought," *The American Scholar* (Spring 1980), 165–166.
10. Ibid.
11. Lyman Abbott, "William Rainey Harper," *Outlook,* no. 82 (January 20, 1906), 110–111; in Frederick Rudolph, *The American College and University: A History* (New York: Alfred A. Knopf, 1962), 356.
12. Christopher Jencks and David Riesman, *The Academic Revolution* (Garden City, NY: Doubleday, 1968), 252.
13. Oscar Handlin, "Epilogue—Continuities," in *Glimpses of the Harvard Past* Bernard Bailyn, Donald Fleming, Oscar Handlin, and Stephan Thernstrom (Cambridge, MA: Harvard University Press, 1986), 131; in Derek Bok, *Universities and the Future of America* (Durham, NC: Duke University Press, 1990), 103.
14. Parker J. Palmer, *To Know as We Are Known* (New York: Harper & Row, 1983).
15. *New York Times* (December 27, 1954), D27.
16. Parker J. Palmer to Russell Edgerton, president of the American Association for Higher Education (April 2, 1990).

The Faculty: A Mosaic of Talent

1. The Carnegie Foundation for the Advancement of Teaching, staff interviews (1989).
2. E. C. Ladd Jr., "The Work Experience of American College Professors: Some Data and an Argument," *Current Issues in Higher Education,* no. 2 (1979); in John M. Braxton and William Toombs, "Faculty Uses of Doctoral Training: Consideration of a Technique for the Differentiation of a Scholarly Effort from Research Activity," *Research in Higher Education,* vol. 16, no. 3 (1982), 266.
3. The Carnegie Foundation for the Advancement of Teaching, "Professoriate Prose: Hieroglyphics from Higher Education" (Unpublished collection of quotations from the survey instruments of the 1989 National Survey of Faculty), 17.

4. The Carnegie Foundation for the Advancement of Teaching, staff interviews (1989).
5. Ibid.
6. Ernest L. Boyer, personal conversation (August 24 1990).
7. The Carnegie Foundation for the Advancement of Teaching, staff interviews (1989).
8. Ibid.
9. Mary Ellen Elwell, letter to *The Chronicle of Higher Education* (September 5, 1990), B3.
10. Syracuse University, "Writing Program: Promotion and Tenure Guidelines" (Unpublished draft, December 14, 1989), 2.
11. Kenneth E. Eble, "The Aims of College Teaching" (Speech delivered at the Leadership Development Seminar, Central State University, Edmond, OK, September 24, 1985; reprinted in the *1985–1986 Annual Report of the Oklahoma Network of Continuing Higher Education*), 9; in Ernest L. Boyer, *College: The Undergraduate Experience in America* (New York: Harper & Row, 1987), 138–139.

The Creativity Contract

1. Henry David Thoreau, *Walden and Civil Disobedience*, ed. Owen Thomas (New York: W. W. Norton, 1966), 213.
2. L. Lee Knefelkamp, "Seasons of Academic Life," *Liberal Education*, vol. 76, no. 3 (May–June 1990), 4.
3. Roger G. Baldwin and Robert T. Blackburn, "The Academic Career as a Developmental Process," *Journal of Higher Education*, vol. 52, no. 6 (November–December 1981), 599; citing Daniel Levinson et al., *The Seasons of a Man's Life* (New York: Alfred A. Knopf, 1978).
4. Frederick Romero, "Aspects of Adult Development," in *Applying Adult Development Strategies*, Mark H. Rossman and Maxine E. Rossman, eds. (New Directions for Adult and Continuing Education, no. 45) (Spring 1990), 4; citing Erik H. Erikson, *Childhood and Society* (New York: W. W. Norton, 1963).
5. Roger G. Baldwin, "Faculty Career Stages and Implications for Professional Development," in *Enhancing Faculty Careers: Strategies for Development and Renewal*, Jack H. Schuster, Daniel W. Wheeler, and Associates, eds. (San Francisco: Jossey-Bass, 1990), 34.
6. Wilbert J. McKeachie, "Perspectives from Psychology: Financial Incentives Are Ineffective for Faculty," in *Academic Rewards in Higher*

Education, D. R. Lewis and W. E. Becker Jr., eds. (Cambridge, MA: Ballinger, 1979), 14.

7. Baldwin, *Enhancing Faculty Careers,* 24.
8. Carolyn J. Mooney, "Faculty Generation Gap Brings Campus Tensions, Debates over Rating of Professors," *The Chronicle of Higher Education* (June 27, 1990), A 19.
9. The Carnegie Foundation for the Advancement of Teaching, "Professoriate Prose: Hieroglyphics from Higher Education" (Unpublished collection of quotations from the survey instruments of the 1989 National Survey of Faculty), 29.

The Campuses: Diversity with Dignity

1. Clark Kerr, *The Uses of the University, with a "Postscripts 1972"* (Cambridge, MA: Harvard University Press, 1972), 86.
2. David Riesman, *Constraint and Variety in American Education* (Lincoln: University of Nebraska Press, 1956), 14.
3. The Carnegie Foundation for the Advancement of Teaching, 1989 National Survey of Faculty.
4. Ernest A. Lynton and Sandra E. Elman, *New Priorities for the University* (San Francisco: Jossey-Bass, 1987), 13.
5. The Carnegie Foundation for the Advancement of Teaching and the American Council on Education, National Survey of College and University Presidents (1989); in The Carnegie Foundation for the Advancement of Teaching, *Campus Life* (Princeton, NJ: Author, 1990), Appendix A, Table A-7.
6. Christopher Jencks and David Riesman, *The Academic Revolution* (Garden City, NY: Doubleday, 1968), 531–532.
7. The Carnegie Foundation for the Advancement of Teaching, staff interview (1989).
8. The Carnegie Foundation for the Advancement of Teaching, College Visits (1984–1985); in Ernest L. Boyer, *College: The Undergraduate Experience in America* (New York: Harper & Row, 1987), 127.
9. Kenneth Ruscio, "The Distinctive Scholarship of the Selective Liberal Arts College," *Journal of Higher Education;* vol. 58, no. 2 (March–April 1987), 214.
10. American Association of Community and Junior Colleges, *Building Communities: A Vision for a New Century* (A report of the Commission on the Future of Community Colleges) (Washington, DC: National Center for Higher Education, 1988), 7–8.

11. Ibid., 27.
12. George B. Vaughan, "Scholarship: The Community College's Achilles' Heel" (Virginia Community Colleges Association, Occasional Paper Series, Research and Publications Commission, no. 1) (Fall 1989), 5; citing C. Roland Christensen, with Abby J. Hansen, *Teaching and the Case Method* (Boston, MA: Harvard Business School, 1987), 4.
13. Keith Lovin, "AASCU's Role among Institutions of Higher Education," in *Defining the Missions of AASCU Institutions,* John W. Bardo, ed. (Washington, DC: American Association of State Colleges and Universities, 1990), 22.
14. Bruce Henderson and William Kane, letter, *The Chronicle of Higher Education* (May 2, 1990), B3.
15. Thomas R. Lord, "Spotlighting Faculty Scholarship at the Two-Year College," in *Thought and Action: The NEA Higher Education Journal,* vol. 4, no. 2 (1988), 106.
16. Frank F. Wong, "The Ugly Duckling of Higher Education" (Paper presented at the University of the Pacific, Stockton, CA March 30, 1990), 1–2.
17. Ibid., 2.
18. The Carnegie Foundation for the Advancement of Teaching, staff interview (Spring 1990).

A New Generation of Scholars

1. Carnegie Foundation for the Advancement of Teaching, 1989 National Survey of Faculty.
2. William G. Bowen and Julie Ann Sosa, *Prospects for Faculty in the Arts and Sciences* (Princeton, NJ: Princeton University Press, 1989), 216–217.
3. David Riesman, "Can We Maintain Quality Graduate Education in a Period of Retrenchment?" (second David D. Henry Lecture, University of Illinois at Chicago Circle, April 28–29, 1975), 13.
4. Jaroslav Pelikan, *Scholarship and Its Survival: Questions on the Idea of Graduate Education* (Princeton, NJ: Carnegie Foundation for the Advancement of Teaching, 1983), 34.
5. Ernest L. Boyer, *College: The Undergraduate Experience in America* (New York: Harper & Row, 1987), 110.
6. John Henry Newman, *The Idea of a University,* Martin J. Svaglic, ed. with an introduction and notes (Notre Dame, IN: University of Notre Dame Press, 1982), 126.

7. Peter Stanley, "Graduate Education and Its Patrons: Foundations" (Address delivered at 28th annual meeting of the Council of Graduate Schools, Colorado Springs, CO, November 29–December 2, 1988), *CGS Communicator,* vol. 22, no. 1 (1989), 8.
8. G. J. Laing, "The Newer Educational Programs and the Training of Teachers," *The Training of College Teachers,* W. S. Gray, ed. (Chicago: The University of Chicago Press, 1930), 51; in Jody D. Nyquist, Robert D. Abbott, and Donald H. Wulff, "The Challenge of TA Training in the 1990s," in *Teaching Assistant Training in the 1990s,* Nyquist, Abbott, and ed. (New Directions for Teaching and Learning, no. 39) (Fall 1989), 8.
9. Kenneth E. Eble, *Professors as Teachers* (San Francisco: Jossey-Bass, 1972), 180.
10. Robert M. Diamond and Peter Gray, *National Study of Teaching Assistants* (The Center for Instructional Development, Syracuse University) (January 1987), 69.
11. Daniel Fallon, "Truth and the Pendulum" (Presidential Address, Council of Colleges of Arts and Sciences, San Francisco, November 13, 1987), 9.

Scholarship and Community

1. Derek Bok, *Universities and the Future of America* (Durham, NC: Duke University Press, 1990), 105.
2. Ibid.

Afterword

1. M. Kaplan, "Educating for the Common Good: Perspectives on Higher Education for the 21st Century" (Keynote address at the Ernest L. Boyer Center Symposium, Messiah College, Grantham, PA) (2012).
2. E. L. Boyer, *Scholarship Reconsidered: Priorities of the Professoriate* (Princeton, NJ: Carnegie Foundation for the Advancement of Teaching, 1990), 16.
3. Ibid.
4. E. L. Boyer, "The Core Curriculum: A Critique of Uncriticized Assumptions" [Text of paper presented at the Danforth Regional Conference, February 7, 1980] (Catalog No.: 1000 0000 1268, The Ernest L. Boyer, Sr. Archives Collection) (Mechanicsburg, PA: The Ernest L. Boyer Center, Messiah College, 1980).

5. Carnegie Foundation, *Campus Life: In Search of Community* (Princeton, NJ: Author, 1990).
6. E. L. Boyer, *College: The Undergraduate Experience in America* (Princeton, NJ: Carnegie Foundation for the Advancement of Teaching, 1987); E. L. Boyer, "General Education: The Integrated Core" [Text of speech delivered as Academic Convocation Address of the University of San Francisco, April 11, 1988] (Catalog No.: 1000 0000 9298, The Ernest L. Boyer, Sr. Archives Collection) (Mechanicsburg, PA: The Ernest L. Boyer Center, Messiah College, 1988); E. L. Boyer and A. Levine, *A Quest for Common Learning: The Aims of General Education* (Washington, DC: Carnegie Foundation for the Advancement of Teaching, 1981).
7. J. M. Braxton, W. Luckey, and P. Helland, *Institutionalizing a Broader View of Scholarship through Boyer's Four Domains* (San Francisco: Jossey-Bass, 2002); K. O'Meara, "Encouraging Multiple Forms of Scholarship in Faculty Reward Systems: Does It Make a Difference?" *Research in Higher Education,* vol. 46, no. 5 (2005), 479–510.
8. A. M. Rubin, "Is Boyer Misguided or Misused? The Scholarship of Confusion," *Journal of the Association for Communication Administration,* vol. 29 (2000), 260–264.
9. Boyer, *College*; Boyer, "General Education"; Boyer, *Scholarship Reconsidered.*

INDEX